An Invitation *to Die*

To Anna!
Live Free!
Marie Sheek

An Invitation to Die

A Woman's Pursuit of Authentic Faith

Marie Shull

WinePressPublishing
Great Books, Defined.

WinePress Publishing (PO Box 428, Enumclaw, WA 98022) functions only as book publisher. As such, the ultimate design, content, editorial accuracy, and views expressed or implied in this work are those of the author.

Unless otherwise noted, Scripture references are taken from the *Holy Bible, New International Version*®, *NIV*®. Copyright © 1973, 1978, 1984 by Biblica, Inc.™ Used by permission of Zondervan. All rights reserved worldwide. www.zondervan.com

Scripture references marked NKJV are taken from the *New King James Version*. Copyright © 1982 by Thomas Nelson, Inc. Used by permission. All rights reserved.

Scripture references marked KJV are taken from the *King James Version* of the Bible.

Scripture references marked NLT are taken from the *Holy Bible, New Living Translation*, copyright © 1996, 2004, 2007 by Tyndale House Foundation. Used by permission of Tyndale House Publishers, Inc., Carol Stream, Illinois 60188. All rights reserved.

Scripture references marked NASB are taken from the *New American Standard Bible*, © 1960, 1963, 1968, 1971, 1972, 1973, 1975, 1977 by The Lockman Foundation. Used by permission.

ISBN 13: 978-1-4141-1839-0
ISBN 10: 1-4141-1839-2
Library of Congress Catalog Card Number: 2010907970

Contents

༄

PART THREE: PUTTING ON THE NEW SELF

PART FOUR: FINDING YOUR FIT

Preface

IT WAS EARLY June, and my husband and I were on a return visit to Africa with a short-term mission team. I was walking back to the mission guesthouse after another discouraging encounter with the headmaster of the Christian school where we were attempting to build a library and resource center. Funds were missing, and the explanations were becoming more creative and less believable. I grumbled to God, "How can we build trust in this culture when our own Christian brothers lie, cheat, and steal?"

I was in the middle of this whining session when I walked into the dining room at the guesthouse and met a young Peace Corps worker from Ohio named Kapree. She had been assigned to our school and had a passion to see a library built there, so we had an instant connection. As we talked, I gleaned a clear picture of her liberal, secular worldview. What a great opportunity to "testify to the truth."

Over the next several weeks, I shared with her a few fundamentals of the Christian faith. Near the end of my stay, the two of us were on a bus heading to the bank in a nearby town. It gave me a chance to talk about what the life of an authentic disciple of Christ could look like. Her response pierced my soul. She said, "If that is what an authentic Christian is, then I have never met one!"

How is that possible? Why are we not making an impact in our culture? If we are "Christ's ambassadors," why are we not representing Him authentically? Then the Holy Spirit reminded me of my own journey from feminism to marginal faith, where I had wallowed in spiritual mediocrity for years. It was humbling indeed!

Introduction

SEVERAL YEARS AGO, I was invited to speak at a women's retreat in Myrtle Beach, South Carolina. I was thrilled to accept the invitation because the Lord had placed a message on my heart that I was eager to share.

But how do you invite a hundred women to a retreat called "An Invitation to Die" and expect that you will have an overflow crowd? So we called it "Christ in You; the Hope of Glory" (Col. 1:27). Only after we had everyone in the conference room, and had locked the doors, did we reveal the true title.

The women received the theme with a little laughter and a lot of curiosity. Over the weekend, it became obvious to me that the message of "dying to self" was not often heard from the pulpits of our self-absorbed culture. After the retreat, I was convinced of the magnitude of this message for today's Christian women. Author and editor Gene Edwards shares his view that: ". . . from a purely historical viewpoint, we must be categorized as the most universally shallow believers ever to cross the pages of history."[1] I began to pray about what God would have me do next, and this book is the result.

What does it mean to live the "crucified life," and why are so few of us following that spiritual path? A. W. Tozer writes in *The Root of the Righteous*, "Millions of professed believers talk as if He (Christ) were real and act as if He were not."[2] Why? What have we missed?

Wesley Duewel, in his book *Measure Your Life*, says, "A self-filled Christian is the opposite of a Spirit-filled Christian. To be filled with the Spirit is the secret of spiritual success and growth. To be filled with self is the cause of spiritual defeat. There is no risen life in the Spirit until there is a crucifixion of the self-life."[3]

Scripture describes it this way: "I have been crucified with Christ and I no longer live, but Christ lives in me. The life I live in the body I live by faith in the Son of God, who loved me and gave himself for me" (Gal. 2:20). Most believers will not experience this level of faith and obedience or the joy and peace that come only through surrender.

Have you wallowed in spiritual mediocrity for years as I had? Then I invite you to die—to put to death whatever belongs to your earthly nature (Col. 3:5) and live in the power and abiding presence of the living God. It would be my privilege to serve as your discipleship coach in your quest for the "crucified life."

In Part One, I'll share my own journey from liberal feminist with an attitude to surrendered and joy-filled disciple of Christ called into leadership of women's ministry. I will hold nothing back, because freedom in Christ allows us to live authentically—with nothing to hide, nothing to prove, and nothing to lose. Then I will ask you to reflect on your own story.

In Part Two, we will walk together through the process of "taking off the old self"—surrendering your own worldview, wounds, wants, and will. It will conclude with a parable that illustrates this process of surrender.

In Part Three, you will begin the process of "putting on the new self" as you strive to nurture your spirit through the Word, prayer, worship, and service—becoming "filled to the measure of all the fullness of God" (Eph. 3:19). We will explore the roles we fulfill as we live in authentic faith: as an ambassador of Christ, an advocate for the church, and an activist in the community.

In Part Four, we will identify your personality, values, passions, abilities, and spiritual gifts in order to create a vision of your unique place of service in the kingdom of God.

At the end of each chapter in Parts Two, Three, and Four, you will find one or more suggested action steps for you to take, a question for reflection, and a prayer. I hope that these help you to process the material in a way that is helpful for you and leads you on the transformed journey you will have begun.

I cannot promise that this book will transform your life, for true change comes through the transforming power of the Holy Spirit, but I do believe that as you surrender your self-stuff and pursue Him with passion and purpose, you will experience the "abundant life."

How to Get the Most out of this Book

There are several ways to work through this book:

- Independently—you can choose to go through the entire book on your own with the help of the Holy Spirit.
- With a trusted friend—you can encourage each other to dig deeper in honest self-reflection and pray together for the strength to face issues that may have been buried long ago.

- In a small group—you can use this book as a small group study that meets regularly for discussion, prayer, and encouragement.

Regardless of the option you select as you work through the material the first time, it is my hope and prayer that you will use this book as a resource to mentor or coach another person again and again. You will find additional coaching concepts, tools, and techniques in the appendix at the end of the book.

However you choose to proceed, you will need your Bible; a journal; time; and a quiet place to ponder, pray, and process all that the Holy Spirit will reveal to you. This process is not magical; it is biblical. It is not pop psychology but spiritual obedience. I pray that you will hunger and thirst for this deeper life and accept His invitation to die—that you might truly live.

Part One

The Power of a Story

Your story has power in your own life, and it has power and meaning to bring to others. I want your story to stir me, draw me to tears, compel me to ask hard questions. I want to enter your heartache and join you in the hope of redemption. But your story can't do these things if you can't tell it. You can't tell your story until you know it. And you can't truly know it without owning your part in writing it. And you won't write a really glorious story until you've wrestled with the Author who has already written long chapters of your life, many of them not to your liking.

—Dan Allender, *To Be Told*[1]

The Death of Innocence

MY NINTH YEAR marked the death of innocence and the birth of hatred. I was the eldest of four children, and Mother was pregnant with number five. She was a woman of simple, childlike faith. Dad was rarely home. After his shift at the factory in a blue-collar suburb of Detroit, he headed straight to his favorite bar, and we seldom saw him. When he did come home, I often found a place to hide and pray that he would leave or pass out soon. He was a mean-spirited drunk. I never wandered far from home. I felt an intense need to protect Mom from his abuse.

On one typical evening at home without Dad, the younger kids were playing in the back bedroom and I was reading—my favorite means of escape—when Mom yelled for me. She was always so soft-spoken that her scream took my breath away. I ran to the living room and found her on the floor with a pool of blood between her legs.

"Quick, Marie, grab me a pillow!" she said. As I ran back down the hall, I remember thinking that I couldn't let the little kids see her like that, and I was torn between protecting them and taking care of her. I grabbed a pillow off the nearest bed and ran back as my panic set in. She shoved the pillow between her legs and, in a softer voice, asked me to find Dad. But I stood there, watching in horror as the pillow filled with blood. I felt I couldn't breathe.

Desperate, I pulled the stool up to the wall phone and dialed the number of the bar that Mom had handwritten and taped near the phone. In my hysteria, it was a wonder the bartender understood a single word as I pleaded for him to find my father. An eternity passed before Dad came on the phone.

"Daddy, I think Mommy is dying!" I said desperately. "She's bleeding all over the floor! Oh, Daddy, you gotta come home right now. Please hurry!" There was silence on the other end. Then, with slurred speech, he said something I didn't understand and hung up.

He didn't come! There were no 911 services then, so I called an aunt who lived nearby. She called for an ambulance and then came to stay with us as our world crumpled around us.

Mom lost the baby and so much blood that she remained hospitalized for weeks. We kids were split up among extended family, and for all those weeks apart, no one shared any information about her condition with us.

FILLED WITH FEAR

Terror gripped my gut! It was during those dark, desperate nights that I was sexually molested by two older cousins. I was ashamed, afraid, and so very much alone. Dad became the focus of my anger and hatred.

When the family finally reunited months later, my childhood and innocence were gone. Now I battled to contain the hatred and tried to find ways to escape the looming reality that no one would protect us or comfort us.

When Dad was at home, I couldn't be in the same room with him because my anxiety made me physically sick. I would go to the garage and wait. I watched for hours as spiders spun their webs, waiting and praying that Dad would die. He eventually just walked away, leaving a wife and, by then, five children to fend for themselves.

Mom had only an eighth-grade education and hadn't been employed since her first child was born. We lost our home and were split up once again until our welfare checks started coming. We were able to get a small rental house, and life was better once Dad was gone. We had peace. Poverty, yes, but the peace was wonderful!

Mom could take us to church without ridicule. And take us she did, on the old, rusty, blue church bus every Sunday morning, Sunday night, and Wednesday night. I joined Pioneer Girls, got my very own Bible, and was baptized at age twelve. It was not a particularly spiritual experience. All I could focus on was my white gown. Having lost its weights from the hem, it began rising as I stepped down into the baptismal tank, and I was sure everyone could see my panties. Nevertheless, this became my new identity: the good girl.

Chapter 2

Who Am I, Anyway?

DAN ALLENDER, IN his book *The Wounded Heart*, describes three personas the sexually wounded girl might assume: the "good girl," the "party girl," or the "tough girl." This was, indeed, my "good girl" phase.

THE GOOD GIRL

Life was hard. I watched Mom, with no education or job skills, struggle to meet the needs of her five kids. I often heard her crying, overwhelmed by life. She became increasingly depressed and withdrawn. I remember wondering why she didn't do something about the hole in the roof. When it rained, we just put out the bucket. Eventually, we just adapted to walking around the bucket. We learned to fend for ourselves at mealtimes when there was food in the cupboard, and when we got tired of wearing dirty clothes, we learned to do our own laundry. She never attended PTA meetings or school concerts or offered much in the way of discipline or encouragement. But I never doubted her love.

I made the decision that I would not live that way. I got a job as soon as I could, not only for the money but also to get away from home. I found refuge at school as well and dreamed of better days.

I received a scholarship to college and married Bob, my college sweetheart. We bought a small home in a quiet suburb. It had a white picket fence and petunias blooming in the flower box. I gave birth to our beautiful baby daughter three years into our marriage. We attended church, visited family on weekends, and had hopes of buying a camper to travel during the summer months when Bob was not teaching.

It was a storybook life. I sewed baby clothes from remnant fabric, made homemade cookies for the new cookie jar, and had the exciting challenge of redecorating the bathroom with a budget of $50. I even learned to recover furniture. It was the day of large floral prints in gold, orange, and avocado green. I found the perfect fabric on sale and recovered our sofa, using the leftovers for a tie for Bob. He wore it the day he invited a friend over after school. There he sat, in all his glory, with matching sofa and necktie. Life surely could not get any better than this!

I was off birth control, hoping for another child soon so that our children would be close together in age. We planned for me to teach when the children were old enough for school, and we would spend our summers and school holidays together as a family, perhaps spending weeks at a time at Bob's family's lake cottage in northern Michigan.

I didn't see it coming! Bob walked away from our marriage when our daughter, Kim, was twenty months old. He had been having an affair with one of the teachers at school. My world collapsed. Now what was I going to do?

THE PARTY GIRL

In the early 1970s, the feminist movement permeated the culture. In my pain, I was attracted to its radical agenda, and I began to shed the image of sweet suburban housewife. By 1975, I had sold my house and everything in it, bought one-way tickets to Hawaii for Kim and me (with the hope of applying for graduate school), and begun a new life as a feminist and single mom in paradise.

What a sense of freedom! I knew no one, had no one to whom I was accountable, and began to shed all semblance of restraint. I no longer needed God. I had tried living life His way, and it had only brought greater disappointment and betrayal. Now it would be life on my terms. "I am woman, hear me roar!" Helen Reddy sang my song.

I rented a small, furnished efficiency apartment for a month, until I could secure a job, buy a car, and find childcare for Kim. On our first night in Honolulu, I was tired from the plane trip and emotionally edgy from wondering if I had made a terrible mistake. As I turned on the lights in the kitchen, the sudden splash of brilliance sent an army of *huge* cockroaches scurrying into hiding. When I say huge, I mean *huge*! I screamed, grabbed Kim, and ran out of the apartment into the hall. I marched down to the office, replayed the scene of a few minutes before, and the disinterested clerk merely replied, "Welcome to Hawaii." Kim and I slept together with the lights on that night and many nights afterward.

I began drinking and even tried marijuana once, but I did not like the feeling of being out of control and vulnerable. Men became playthings that I used and tossed away at my discretion. They were never to be trusted. Even the physician who offered me a job at Queens Hospital in Honolulu let it be known that there were sexual strings attached. No thanks! It was life on my terms, and I was not about to walk into that bondage. There had to be other options.

I found a job at St. Francis Hospital, enrolled Kim in a Montessori preschool, and found a rental house to share with another single mother. We settled into a new way of life—one without family, familiar friends, or faith. I did go to church on Easter and Christmas that year. Old habits die hard.

When I was not at work, Kim and I spent many hours at the beach, usually searching for stretches of sand away from crowds. I had signed up for a photography class at the YMCA, and these trips to the beach became my favorite photo opportunities. While Kim built castles in the sand, I captured her from every angle. She was creative, cute, and confident. As her trusting, sea-blue eyes came into focus through my viewfinder, I wondered what would become of us.

No one had warned me that the cost of living in Hawaii was not sustainable on one income. Each month I dipped into the savings from the sale of our house. At this rate, I would be out of money by the end of the year and wouldn't even have enough for a one-way ticket home. My dream of remaining in Hawaii until I could finish graduate school was dying quickly. So with a bit of regret mixed with a pinch of relief, I made the decision to return to Michigan.

We settled in the Ann Arbor area because a nearby hospital had offered me a job. It was early summer, and the position would not be available until after Labor Day. My ex-husband, Bob, and his parents asked if Kim could spend six weeks with them since she had been in Hawaii with me the previous year. Though Bob was not the most attentive father, his mother was absolutely crazy about her first grandchild, and I could not deny her request. But what would I do with six weeks without a job and without Kim?

I had a little savings left. How about a backpacking trip to Europe? I invited a girlfriend from Hawaii to go with me. It was quite an adventure—youth hostels, European rail passes, and when all else failed, hitchhiking. I had a brief affair with an Irish gent I met in Dublin. He was on his way to London for a business meeting, and I agreed to meet him at his hotel. I hadn't expected a doorman in red velvet tails to scrutinize me before allowing me access to the lobby. I was braless and wearing a denim jumper with a rather risqué view of my navel. I was hauling a large backpack and wearing hiking sandals that looked as if they had just run through muddy pasture land. I didn't blame the guy for his disdain, but I just wanted to get to the room for a hot shower. I can't even remember what story I told him. I'm sure he didn't believe any of it. He eventually called the room for confirmation, and I headed into the lobby with a haughty grin.

Weeks later, I met a German fellow in Heidelberg who turned out to be a "one-night stand." Each time I gave myself away, I sensed the hole in my soul growing deeper and darker, but I justified it, believing that any guilt I was feeling was leftover bondage from an unenlightened age of Victorian morals, no longer relevant in the "Age of Aquarius." Sexual freedom—it was simply expected from a liberal feminist.

I returned home Labor Day weekend with a $50 traveler's check and an empty savings account. A message awaited me. The woman who was leaving the position I had been offered had chosen not to resign because her plans for graduate school had fallen through.

I did not have a job! Fall was fast approaching, and Kim was entering kindergarten. I had sold all our fall and winter clothes, shoes, coats, and boots before moving to Hawaii. I had no choice but to replace our winter wardrobe using a charge card. Grocery stores, however, did not accept credit cards in those days. So Kim and I ate every meal in restaurants that would take Visa. We took the leftovers home, and I packed them for her lunch the next day.

The bills mounted up fast. The rent and car payment were overdue. I had no one I could ask for a loan. In all honesty, I was probably far too prideful to ask, even if I had had the opportunity. Finally, in November, I accepted a promising position at the Veterans Administration hospital in Ann Arbor. It took nearly four years to pay off that Visa bill!

Ann Arbor, the liberal Mecca of the Midwest, was the perfect "hothouse" for a budding feminist: cocktail parties with the university crowd, clandestine affairs with university faculty, and out-of-state conferences with opportunities to meet men from all over the country—intelligent, successful, charming men, who usually were married.

Several years later, I took a position as a technical director at the University Medical Center, developed an allied-health training program in vascular ultrasound, and became the national president of our professional society.

It was the late 1970s, and I was returning home from a medical conference in Ohio, somewhat lonely, but filled with a sense of self-importance, when I met Marc, a young, Jewish medical sales associate who was waiting to board the same plane. It was a magnetic attraction. We fell desperately in love. Well, I called it love then, but lust is probably more honest. I let all those years of guarding my heart fall away like autumn leaves in a blustery wind. Being apart was painful. He pledged his undying love, and we began to make plans for a life together. Life had a bubbling—no, a boiling excitement that I could barely contain.

Then, with very little warning of what was to come, Marc confessed that he already was married with two children and his company was moving him and his family to California. I was beyond devastated—I was numb. How could I have been so blind, so vulnerable, and so foolish? I couldn't sleep, eat, or work for days. But when I emerged from that emotional cave, I was different. I was tough, bitter, and biting.

THE TOUGH GIRL

I was done with men! I developed friendships with other single mothers, and we spent a lot of our time together verbally beating up on men, but that got old after awhile, and I was ready to move on. My focus became my daughter and my work. I had very few friends, for I trusted no one. I resolved to remain single the rest of my life. Kim became my sole purpose for living. I would be her protector and provider, the most perfect parent. It was the two of us against the world!

A New World

I HAD BEEN single for seven years by the time I met Ken. I thought I had made peace with the fact that I would never remarry. I was speaking at a medical conference, and he approached me afterwards and invited me for further discussion over a cup of coffee. He seemed like a nice guy, more humble than the typical surgeon I had worked with over the years. Our conversation remained on a professional level, and a few days later, I was back on a plane, heading home.

Months later, I was attending a conference in California, and this guy was waving at me from across the auditorium. During the break, he found me and acted as if we were old friends. Frankly, I barely remembered Ken. He invited me to go sailing in San Diego Bay with some friends of his. I love to sail. It was a natural connection. I said "yes" but remained very cautious.

Ken was a kind, attentive, Southern gentleman, but he was in the last days of an unhealthy marriage, and I was not about to get tangled up in that. Besides, I was returning home in a few days, and that would be the end of it. Ken, however, had other thoughts. Suffice it to say, Ken is very tenacious. He began calling me regularly and finding excuses to see me. Between airfare and phone bills, this budding relationship was costing him dearly.

He began to drop hints about me moving to North Carolina, where he had accepted a position with a surgical private practice. I was reluctant. I had so much at stake! But he pressed on, talking about how it would be a wonderful place to raise Kim, we could work together, and eventually we would become a family. My defenses were weakening.

Six months after we met, I left my position in Ann Arbor, and Kim and I moved south. Not just south, but to a small, conservative, southern town in the middle of the "Bible Belt." Talk about culture shock!

It was 1980, and the Ku Klux Klan made headlines in the local newspaper. Neighborhoods were segregated by race, and women were not allowed during the lunch hour at the dinner club where Ken's practice had a membership. This was not a good fit for a liberal feminist! I felt like I was in a time warp. I would never fit in here!

I remember the first cocktail party we attended. I was wearing a simple, Indian cotton sundress. Ken looked at me curiously. "Are you wearing that?"

"I had planned to. Is there a problem?" I said as I looked at him with a defiant air.

"Well, you might feel a bit under-dressed," he said. I could sense his concern.

"I'll be fine, really," I said. I had no idea that women still dressed in chiffon, wore skinny high-heeled sandals, and had painted toenails. But that was not my biggest shock. Every guest at the party was white, and every one of the wait staff was black, dressed in organdy aprons and carrying silver trays. And no one else seemed to notice! I looked at Ken to see his reaction. He seemed perfectly at home in this environment.

I wanted to leave and head back to Ann Arbor, where I understood the culture. But Ken was very kind and comforting, promising me that things were changing, even in the South.

Ken and I moved in together before his divorce was final. We were the scandal of the medical community. I have to admit now that I rather enjoyed the shock we created. I was brazen, brash, and braless! However, I did realize that in order to survive in the south, I would have to clean up my image, at least a little. We moved into a traditional, professional neighborhood; joined the country club; and attended a large, mainline church where many young professionals could be found on Sunday morning dressed in their designer clothes and sitting in their "reserved" pews with their beautiful families. What was I doing here?

ANOTHER TRY AT MARRIAGE

Ken and I lived together a full year before we married. Kim was nine years old at the time and served as our lone wedding attendant. We were married in the chapel of the church on a Friday evening after teaching together in medical seminars all week. We wrote our own wedding vows, and I made sure there was nothing about a wife submitting to her husband and surely no mention of the "till death do us part" promise. I had no illusions that this marriage would last a lifetime; it was only a matter of time. However, I was willing to engage this phase as long as it lasted.

I worked hard to fit into this new community for Ken's sake. It was important to his practice. But I was struggling. I had grown up in a culture that valued honesty to a fault. I was now living in a culture that valued courtesy and graciousness well above honesty, and I struggled to figure out what people were truly saying. There are subtle communication rules that southern women know, but I did not. And the rules become more complex when you add the Bible Belt expectations of image and behavior.

Generally, these are the rules as I began to perceive them:

1. *Always* speak "nice-nice."
2. Tell people *only* what they want to hear.
3. *Never, ever* reveal any issues that might tarnish the family image.

I was indeed struggling.

THE FAMILY EXPANDS

Ken and I had been trying to have a child since we were married, as we were now in our thirties. After many disappointing months and discouraging fertility evaluations, we came to accept the fact that we would not conceive. It was 1982, and we were preparing for our first medical mission trip to Bolivia. I was going, but with a poor attitude.

We were a team of eleven, and as I began to add up the expenses, I said, "Isn't it more rational just to send the money? Think of all the things they could do with $25,000!" In my quiet thoughts, which I did not voice, I believed that these people were merely a bunch of "goody-goodies" who would go on this adventure, take lots of pictures, and come home to tell everyone who would listen the wonderful things they were doing for God. I really wanted no part of it. But Ken wanted us to experience it together, so to foster peace in my marriage, I went along.

At that time in Bolivia, there was an overwhelming number of orphans, and many of them did not live to see their fifth birthdays. I thought I had found the perfect solution to grow our family: international adoption. On our return home, we began to investigate our options but did not find an international adoption agency in North Carolina. Instead, we applied to adopt children within the state—older sibling groups of up to three children. We waited two years without a phone call.

In the spring of 1984, Ken and I were attending a Sunday evening class at the church. In another room down the hall, a local obstetrician talked about abortion. I wanted to hear what he had to say, so I slipped in a few minutes late and took a seat in the back row. After the open discussion time, I went to him and shared our desire to adopt. He said that he had not delivered an adoptable baby in years. Most of the healthy ones the mothers kept, and those who were crack cocaine babies or those of alcoholic mothers often were aborted. He assured me that we would not want to adopt one of them anyway. At the time, that sounded very logical and humane.

The very next day, a young woman walked into this same obstetrician's office. She was five months pregnant and wanted to find a family to adopt her baby. She was a sweet, innocent, young girl with no history of drugs or alcohol. We got the call that would change our lives.

Shock, delight, fear! What if there is something wrong with the baby? Could I love this child as I loved my own? Am I too old at thirty-six? Would the birth mother try to get the baby back?

We chose to meet the birth mother, made arrangements for a private adoption, and brought Geoffrey home from the hospital when he was two days old. What an incredible gift! He was beautiful, healthy, and the perfect addition to complete our family, binding us closer together. Could life get any better?

A Mother's Nightmare

EACH SUMMER, KIM was required, by court order, to spend at least two weeks with her father in Michigan. I was reluctant to let her go after her grandmother passed away. Bob was struggling with alcohol, and his life was quickly spiraling out of control. He was disengaged as a father, and he rarely knew where Kim was when I called to check on her. It was an unhealthy environment, ripe for disaster.

And sure enough, disaster befell my daughter. Kim was raped during her summer visit the year she was thirteen. When she got home, I knew something had happened. She was different. She was withdrawn, angry, and defiant, but she denied that anything specific had happened. Her grades began to drop, her friends changed, and her demeanor darkened. I wanted to believe that it was just a phase. I tried hard not to pry, but I was scared.

Then she was arrested for shoplifting, which began a plunge into outright rebellion. When she went off to college, I felt some relief from the stress, but it was short-lived. She was partying so much that she finally just quit going to classes. We were forced to make one of the toughest decisions I have ever had to make. We cut off her financial support. She lost her apartment and began sleeping at a friend's place.

I was emotionally exhausted from all the drama. I went to see our pastor and shared the pain of my heart as a mother. "I feel like we are in a battle for the soul of my child, and I don't know what to do," I said.

His response to me was, "Well, what do you want me to do about it?" No compassion, no prayer, no hope.

I was defeated. I had tried everything I knew to do. Her life choices were destroying me and creating a huge conflict in our marriage. I still had no idea what had begun her spiral into darkness. Shame caused her to hold onto that secret until she was nineteen.

MORE BETRAYAL

When she finally felt she could be honest with me, what she shared broke my heart. Though the rape was damaging enough in itself, the most painful part was her father's reaction. It was late at night, and he was "high" on drugs and alcohol. Kim went to him, hysterically revealing what had happened. He told her to go on to bed and they would deal with it in the morning. No compassion! No comfort! Never even bothered to get out of bed. And it was not dealt with in the morning, or ever. So Kim just buried the pain, and the darkness engulfed her.

When Kim became pregnant at twenty-one, she decided to marry the father, an agnostic with a temper and an alcohol problem. I pleaded with her not to marry him. We would help her and the baby, and she could go back to school and finish her education. But she insisted that she wanted her child to have an intact family. We planned a small wedding at the same chapel where Ken and I were married. Then when Kim was seven months pregnant, her husband became involved with another woman and sent Kim packing. She came home broken, bitter, and barely able to function.

We made a home for Kim in a basement apartment and prepared for the birth of our first grandchild. Our mother-daughter relationship was beyond strained—it was fractured. She did not want to be there, and frankly, I didn't want her there. But we had a grandchild on the way, and I could not put her out on the street.

Kim stayed with us through the birth of our grandson, Zachary, and for six weeks afterward. It was a hard time for both of us. She was understandably ill-equipped emotionally to handle motherhood, and she resented my role in nurturing her son.

When Zachary was six weeks old, Kim's husband wanted his wife and child back home and wanted us out of their lives. He eventually moved them to Maine, and I had very little contact with them.

Chapter 5

The Search for Hope

I HAD COME to the end of my own ability to handle life. If there was any hope for Kim, any hope for me, I had to find it. Scripture says, "You will seek me and find me when you seek me with all of your heart" (Jer. 29:13).

Our son, Geoff, was attending a Christian school that seemed to offer something more substantial spiritually than anything I previously had experienced. So we visited the church that was associated with his school. It was very different, indeed. The pastor used the Bible when he preached. In the worship service, there was a reverence for God, but it was balanced with an intimacy with the Lord that I never had known or believed possible. I became like one dying of thirst, and after seeing a glimpse of the pool of life-giving water, I ran with abandon toward life and truth.

Jesus said, "If anyone is thirsty, let him come to me and drink. Whoever believes in me, as the scripture has said, streams of living water will flow from within him (John 7:37–38).

QUENCHING MY THIRST

I went to the local Christian bookstore and bought a new Bible—a big one, with lots of study guides and open spaces for taking notes. I was determined to find *real* Christianity. In our previous church, I had been teaching adult Sunday school, singing in the choir, and serving on the missions committee, but my prayers were shallow and self-serving, and I rarely spent time in God's Word. As I understood it then, the Old Testament was simply the history of the Jewish nation, and the New Testament was a guidebook on how to be kind and loving to one another, nothing more. I had so much yet to learn!

I began taking every Bible study I could fit into my schedule. I bought a book on prayer by E. M. Bounds and *The Pursuit of God* by A. W. Tozer. I began to get a vision of what authentic Christianity looked like. And I wanted it more than life itself. Then I began to read some troubling passages: "If anyone would come after me, he must deny himself and take up his cross daily and follow me" (Luke 9:23). "Anyone who does not take his cross and follow me is not worthy of me" (Matt. 10:38). "And anyone who does not carry his cross and follow me cannot be my disciple" (Luke 14:27).

TAKING UP MY CROSS

I realized that unless I took up my cross and followed Him, I was not worthy of Him and could not be called a disciple of Christ. I asked, "Lord, please help me to understand what this means! I am to carry this cross, but for what purpose? As far as I know, there is only one purpose for the cross—crucifixion. Lord, what are you asking?"

A. W. Tozer explains it this way: "We must do something about the cross, and one of two things only we can do—flee it or die upon it . . . . To do this is to submit the whole pattern of our lives to be destroyed and built again in the power of an endless life."[1]

Jesus took up His cross in obedience to His Father, surrendering His life to save mine. I had come truly to believe that. But believing and behaving are not the same. Another Tozer quote brought me face-to-face with a bold, penetrating reality.

> The essence of my belief is that there is a difference, a vast difference between fact and truth. Truth in the Scriptures is more than a fact. A fact may be detached, impersonal, cold, and totally disassociated from life. Truth on the other hand, is warm, living, and spiritual. A theological fact may be held in the mind for a lifetime without its having any positive effect on the moral character, but truth is creative, saving, transforming, and it always changes the one who receives it into a humbler and holier man [or woman]. At what point, then, does a theological fact become for the one who holds it a life-giving truth? At that point where obedience begins.[2]

I wanted desperately to understand what this meant practically. How do we live the crucified life every day? How do we even begin? For me, it had to begin with a confrontation with my worldview, which was far from biblical.

I Can Do It Myself, Thank You

I WAS A liberal feminist, and my worldview, or as the Bible calls it, my "worldly wisdom," was completely out of alignment with God's Word. I had left the faith of my youth and put my trust in education, self-sufficiency, and "the pursuit of happiness." I believed that I was the ultimate authority over my life. I could determine my values, my plans, my dreams, my morals, and my future. I had beaten the odds. I had overcome poverty, ignorance, abuse, abandonment, and adultery. I was in control of my life. I was arrogant and critical of anyone who was not an "overcomer."

I remember a conversation I had with an associate pastor at our new church, just weeks after transferring our membership. I told him I did not have a humble bone in my body and that I was proud of it! Though I said it in jest, there was far too much truth in that statement.

DEBATING WITH GOD

Let's look at what Scripture has to say about the wisdom of the world. I've included a sampling of my own raw, but very real, thoughts as I began the quest for truth.

"The fear of the Lord is the beginning of wisdom, and the knowledge of the Holy One is understanding" (Prov. 9:10). I wondered, *What is this fear of the Lord? I thought Christianity was all about love.*

"Where is the wise man? Where is the scribe? Where is the debater of this age? Has not God made foolish the wisdom of the world?" (1 Cor. 1:20). *Wait a minute*, I thought. *Isn't it the Bible-thumping Christian who appears foolish?*

"See to it that no one takes you captive through philosophy and empty deception, according to the tradition of men, according to the elementary principles of this world, rather than according to Christ" (Col. 2:8). *No one holds me captive!* I thought. *I am a free thinker—educated, competent, and aware.*

"For whatever is born of God overcomes the world: and this is the victory that has overcome the world—our faith. Who is the one who overcomes the world, but he who believes that Jesus is the Son of God?" (1 John 5:4–5). Again, in my mind, I challenged these words. *That's not been my experience. The few faithful Christians I have known have been beaten down by the world—exploited, abused, and abandoned. They didn't look very victorious to me!*

> For the grace of God has appeared, bringing salvation to all men, instructing us to deny ungodliness and worldly desires and to live sensibly, righteously and godly in the present age, looking for the blessed hope and the appearing of the glory of our great God and Savior, Christ Jesus, who gave Himself for us to redeem us from every lawless deed, and to purify for Himself a people for His own possession, zealous for good deeds.
>
> —Titus 2:11–13 (NASB)

Come on, isn't this a little unrealistic? I asked myself again. *Look around! How many sensible, righteous, and godly people do you know in this present age? And this thought about being God's own possession? Well, that's a pretty big risk. I'm not sure I want to be anyone's possession. That seems reminiscent of the old "woman as property" mentality.*

"My purpose is that they may be encouraged in heart and united in love, so they may have the full riches of complete understanding, in order that they may know the mystery of God, namely Christ, in whom are hidden all the treasures of wisdom and knowledge" (Col. 2:2–3). Again I questioned this in my mind: *If all the treasures of wisdom and knowledge are hidden in Christ, why do all the Christians seem to be the most naïve, narrow-minded, and uninformed gathering of people in a community?*

> As for you, you were dead in your transgressions and sins, in which you used to live when you followed the ways of this world and of the ruler of the kingdom of the air, the spirit who is now at work in those who are disobedient. All of us also lived among them at one time, gratifying the cravings of our sinful nature and following its desires and thoughts. Like the rest, we were by nature objects of wrath.
>
> —Ephesians 2:1–3

Again, I thought, *I was an object of wrath? Well, I know I'm not Mother Teresa, but an object of wrath? That seems rather harsh. Am I deceived by the philosophy of this world? I thought I was just enlightened. And as for gratifying the cravings of our "sinful" nature and following its desires and thoughts—well, we are just human, after all!*

"Do not conform any longer to the pattern of this world, but be transformed by the renewing of your mind. Then you will be able to test and approve what God's will is—his good, pleasing and perfect will" (Rom. 12:2).

I found myself at a crossroads. I knew I had come to the time when I had to accept the truth of Scripture—all of it—or reject it as unenlightened dogma of a bygone era. I no longer could pick and choose from the Bible what I wanted to believe. It was either truth or it wasn't. All or nothing! This would be the biggest decision of my life. If I chose Scripture as the fundamental truth, I would have to rethink everything.

- I didn't like the fact that Jesus was the only way to God (John 14:6). It seemed so exclusive.
- I didn't like what the Bible said about divorce (Matthew 19:3–9). It seemed so Victorian and irrelevant.
- And what about this talk of unconditional love? (1 Cor. 13:1–13). I didn't believe it really could exist.

It was a battle for my mind—and for my heart. This pursuit of authentic Christianity was too uncomfortable. Maybe it would be easier to go back to our old church and find comfort in the shallow end, where spiritual complacency was familiar and nonthreatening. We could pick up where we left off, and maybe learn to wear the mask with more finesse.

But in the end, I knew there was no going back. What if it is all true? What if we really could know the mystery of God in Christ, in whom are hidden all the treasures of wisdom and knowledge? What if I could learn to accept for myself this unconditional love and then learn to give it? I didn't have all the answers, but like the apostle Peter, I thought, *Where else can I go? Perhaps Christ alone holds the words to eternal life* (John 6:68).

A Choice for Life

I CHOSE TRUTH and life! I chose to accept Scripture as the inerrant Word of God, the foundational truth that would become the filter for every aspect of my worldview. I had to confess both my ignorance and my arrogance. I repented of my smug disobedience and pleaded for forgiveness for my sins. It was a very humbling experience to go from enlightened feminist to wretched sinner; from self-sufficiency to total dependency. In my prayer time, even now, I often begin by acknowledging God's sovereignty over all of life and His authority over mine. I need the reminder every now and then.

So how did accepting Scripture as truth alter my feminist worldview? It totally dismantled it. For example:

- I was not my own! I had been bought with a price (1 Cor. 6:19–20).
- I was not simply a feminist with a progressive attitude toward sexual freedom. I was a sinner (2 Cor. 12:21).
- My arrogance and self-sufficiency were not badges of honor. God detests and opposes the proud, and they will not go unpunished (Prov. 16:15; 1 Pet. 5:5).
- I was not the final authority over my life. One day, every knee will bow and every tongue will confess that Jesus Christ is Lord (Phil. 2:10–11).
- I don't have to strive, in my own strength, to clean up my life. He Who began a good work in me will perfect it until the day Jesus returns (Phil. 1:6).

And the dismantling continues. As the Holy Spirit reveals His truth, I have a choice to surrender another nugget of "worldly wisdom," to be crucified, or to cling to it with all the tenacity that arrogance and ignorance can muster. Thankfully, it's no longer such a struggle but a simple act of obedience, for I've learned to trust Him.

The Hard Road to Forgiveness

A MAJOR BARRIER to living the crucified life is the festering wounds of the past. I thought I had put them behind me, and I did not want to drag them up again. The Holy Spirit, however, had a different agenda.

It was near Father's Day, and the Hallmark commercials played on television. You know how emotionally powerful they can be. Without warning, my eyes began to tear, the lump in my throat swelled to choking proportions, and the sobs followed relentlessly. What was happening to me? This was ridiculous! I had dealt with the abandonment of my father a long time ago, hadn't I? But this pain was so fresh, so overwhelming that I could not deny its realty. Suddenly, I felt as if I couldn't breathe. Was I having an anxiety attack? Was the hatred I had harbored so long beginning to surface and spew forth like hot lava?

PAIN FROM THE PAST

I couldn't imagine being so out of control. Ken was at the hospital, and Geoff was asleep, so I turned off the TV and wept until I was completely spent. I knew what God was showing me: my bitterness toward my father and my unwillingness to forgive. "But, Lord, he does not deserve forgiveness," I told God. "Surely You know that!"

Once again His Word spoke Truth:

Whenever you stand praying, forgive, if you have anything against anyone, so that your Father who is in heaven will also forgive you your transgressions. But if you do not forgive, neither will your Father who is in heaven forgive your transgressions.

—Mark 11:25

Let all bitterness and wrath and anger . . . be put away from you . . . . Be kind to one another, tender-hearted, forgiving each other, just as God in Christ also has forgiven you.

—Ephesians 4:31–32

So, as those who have been chosen of God, holy and beloved, put on a heart of compassion, kindness, humility, gentleness and patience; bearing with one another, and forgiving each other . . . just as the Lord forgave you.

—Colossians 3:12–13

I found myself at another crossroad. I could hold on to the bitterness and become stuck spiritually, or I could surrender it to the cross and find healing and freedom from the pain. But the hole in my soul had been there so long and the scab around it so tough and protective, I wasn't sure I wanted the wound exposed again.

In the early hours of the morning, I finally surrendered my hatred and chose to forgive my father. I wrote him a letter, letting him know that I had forgiven him and hoped he would find peace. We hadn't communicated in over twenty years. I woke in the morning with a weight lifted off my heart and soul. I felt lighter, more joyful than I thought possible.

Several days later, I received a response from my father. His letter said that he had been waiting years to hear from me and he could now find peace. Well, it was one thing to write that letter to an estranged, out-of-state father. It was quite another issue when he asked if he could come to see me. I had to pray long and hard about that!

We did arrange for Dad and his new wife to come for a brief visit. In the past, I couldn't be in the same room with him without getting physically sick. This would certainly be a test of the validity of my forgiveness. Dad and his wife arrived as scheduled, and it was amazing! No pain, no anxiety, no bitterness. Only a subtle sadness for what could have been but what never would be. He was like a distant relative I really didn't know and probably never would. And instead of hatred, there was compassion for him, for his lost soul, for all he had missed, and for his loneliness. He had eleven grandchildren who never had been part of his life.

Several days later, I hugged him goodbye and promised to keep in touch. And I did, until his death years later. All five of his adult children were at his military funeral. It was a healing time for all of us.

PROCESSING THE PAIN

I wish I could tell you that the issue of forgiveness was forever settled for me after that, but that would be a lie. There was still the issue of my relationship with my daughter. After living in Maine for less than a year, Kim called, ten days before Christmas, and said she wanted to come home. Her husband was drinking heavily and becoming violent, and she feared for herself and her son. Ken flew north, rented a moving van, sent Kim and Zachary home on the plane, and drove the truck from Maine through early winter storms. What a great guy!

Eventually, Kim and Zach settled once again in the basement apartment, and Kim enrolled in nursing school. She did not attend church with us, and we didn't push it. We were walking on eggshells around the house, wondering what might set her off again. But it was not Kim who was set off. It was I!

Kim was dropped from the nursing program in her last semester for an incomplete received in an English class. I know that she had turned in the final paper because I had proofed it for her. But she had not followed up on it over the semester break, and the incomplete was converted to an "F." I was in a rage. I spewed ugly words—hurtful words that I couldn't believe were coming from my mouth. It frightened me. Where was this eruption coming from? I was out of control!

I knew that I needed counseling. I made an appointment with a wonderful Christian counselor, who just happened to have a cancellation the next day. When I walked into her office for the first time, thinking *my* issues were all about my relationship with my daughter, the counselor only wanted to talk about my life. I felt frustrated. This was not about me—my daughter was the problem. If she did not pick up on that fact soon, I was not coming back.

The counselor was patient but relentless. Finally, I gave her a brief, unemotional summary of my life, simply so we could get on with the *real* issue. She paused a long time. Had she fallen asleep or lost her train of thought?

Then she made one comment, "You tell that story like it happened to someone else."

I thought about how to respond, but I was not ready to let her peek behind my mask. "Well, maybe it's because I'm not that same little girl. I've grown up, moved on, and I don't dwell on the past."

She asked if she could pray with me before I left. I couldn't wait to get out of there. I wondered if it had been a mistake to come.

Not what I Signed up For

I left her office not intending to return, but there was something compelling about her, and the way she prayed for me was a new experience. She seemed so comfortable and intimate with God. Frankly, it felt a little weird. I went back, and I submitted to her counseling and faithfully completed every assignment she gave me.

One of the first things she had me do was return to my life story—not as a reporter but as a responder. She asked me to go back and relive the truth through the filter of the heart, not the head. She helped me to process the pain and gave me permission to grieve for all the loss. I allowed her to peek behind the mask, and eventually, I felt safe enough to remove it completely. What freedom! Without the limited vision through the mask, I was able to get a glimpse of what healing and wholeness could look like in my life when I experienced freedom in Christ.

With compassion, prayer, and total dependence on the direction of the Holy Spirit, she led me through six months of healing. (Just a side note: Kim was reinstated in the nursing program and graduated with her class.)

Kim was beginning to notice the difference in me, though she thought I was a little weird, becoming a religious fanatic perhaps. Then one Sunday morning, she came upstairs to eat breakfast and appeared to be dressed for church. Ken and I didn't say anything. We acted like it was a normal Sunday ritual. She did come to church that Sunday and most Sundays afterward. After several months, she boldly walked to the altar, shed tears of repentance, and gave her life to Christ. She never went back to the old life. She was born again, a new creation.

Though I thought I had forgiven her for the years of heartbreak, I had a lingering expectation that this new life in Christ was only a phase. I kept looking for signs of the old Kim. I kept expecting her to fall from grace. My heart was guarded, my outlook skeptical, and my comments often critical.

I hated what I was doing, but I couldn't seem to believe fully in her transformation. Our relationship was strained. I decided to make this a prayer priority. For months, I pleaded with God to give me a new vision of Kim as a transformed child of God. I pleaded for a softening of my heart toward her. "Lord, let me see her with your eyes!"

One Saturday, Kim asked if I wanted to go shopping with her. Actually, I was startled that she would want to spend time with me. If I were her, I would not have wanted to spend time with me. However, I agreed and prayed once again that I would not say anything to ruin the day.

THE GIFT OF REDEMPTION

We were on our way home after dark, the windshield wipers lazily brushing away an early evening rain. Kim was listening to a Christian CD and singing along softly. It was a song about redemption. In the light from the oncoming headlights, I noticed tears streaming down her face. She looked toward me and said sadly, "Mom, it doesn't matter what I have done. I've been redeemed."

At that moment, it was as if God opened a window to her soul and allowed me to see her as truly transformed, a redeemed child of God. I couldn't speak; the lump in my throat was too breathtaking and the moment too sacred. My eyes filled with tears as my heart was united with hers for the first time in many years. Nothing more was said that evening, but I knew something was forever changed between us.

Early the next morning, I was on my knees, thanking God for answered prayer. The sobs of gratitude were beyond my control, and I just gave myself over to intense worship and praise. Suddenly, I was compelled to write a poem. Now understand that I am not a poet. But the feeling would not leave. So I got up off my knees, blew my nose, and headed into the kitchen to look for something to write on. I sat down at the counter and simply wrote. The words flowed easily, as if I had memorized them years ago.

> Defiled as a child.
> Rebellion, rage, and running,
> from the only source of healing,
> never kneeling.
> Tough and proud aloud,
> but sobbing in the silence.
> Then a whispered hope, gently calling her near.
> Tenuous and afraid;
> a single tear.
> No longer tough, but not good enough.
> Longing to restore,
> but still keeping score of all the sin that she bore.
> So there she remained,
> not yet free, but no longer chained.
> That's where Abba found her,
> fragile and lost,
> and redeemed her fully that day at the cross.
> Redeemed, transformed, undefiled.
> Once again a pure and precious child!

Immediately I knew what I had been given—a memorial marker to remember the day that the Holy Spirit allowed me to see my daughter as truly redeemed. No, more than redeemed. Redeemed, transformed, and undefiled; once again a pure and precious child. It was amazing!

Then, suddenly, I knew that the poem was also for me. It was my story as well. I couldn't imagine the kind of love that would offer this gift. I was filled to overflowing with it. I ran upstairs and typed the poem on parchment, rolled it as a scroll, and tied a pale blue ribbon around it. I couldn't wait to give it to Kim. It was a gift from the Holy Spirit to both of us and the beginning of a new mother-daughter relationship.

> Give thanks to the Lord, bless His name. The Lord is good; His loving kindness is everlasting and His faithfulness to all generations.
>
> —Psalm 100:4–5

A Path Toward Simplicity

HAVING GROWN UP poor, I felt an undeniable attraction to "the good life." Being married to a surgeon in the South meant that there were certain expectations for our lifestyle, and we complied. Not only did we buy a large, traditional home in the "right" neighborhood and join the country club, but also we purchased a condo at the lake, a sailboat, a foreign sports car, and half ownership in an airplane. We began to travel extensively, often to ski out West or scuba dive in tropical destinations.

As Ken became more successful, the "pleasures of this world" consumed more and more of our time and money. The debt load increased as well, but it didn't seem to bother Ken, so I tried to release it and learn to enjoy what we had acquired. Each time we went on a short-term medical mission trip, the re-entry to our culture and lifestyle created turmoil in my soul. In Bolivia, Haiti, Eastern Europe, Central Asia, and Africa, I learned the difference between what I needed and what I wanted. The accumulation of things, and the debt they created, became much more of a burden than a blessing.

As I began to mature spiritually, my definition of what I wanted began to change dramatically. Rather than "the *good* life," I was in search of the *abundant* life (John 10:10 NKJV). I wondered what Christ was referring to when He talked of the abundant life. Is it something you pursue, or is it the outcome of pursuing Christ? Is there a certain benchmark that lets you know when you've acquired it? Is it the same for everyone, or is there a unique place of peace and contentment for each of us? So many questions, so few simple answers.

In his book *Freedom of Simplicity*, Richard Foster states:

Contemporary culture is plagued by the passion to possess. The unreasoned boast abounds that the good life is found in accumulation, that "more is better." Indeed, we often accept this notion without question, with the result that the lust for affluence in contemporary society has become psychotic: it has completely lost touch with reality. Furthermore, the pace of the modern world accentuates our sense of being fractured and fragmented. We feel strained, hurried, breathless. The complexity of rushing to achieve and accumulate more and more frequently threatens to overwhelm us . . . Christian simplicity frees us from this modern mania. It brings sanity to our compulsive extravagance, and peace to our frantic spirit. . . . Simplicity enables us to live lives of integrity in the face of the terrible realities of our global village.[1]

I remember a comment made by one of my professors during a lecture in an international health class I was attending at a secular university during graduate school in the early 1990s. He talked about the need to live more simply, that others might simply live. I have never forgotten the power of that phrase from the mouth of a secular humanist. If this is true for the secular humanist, how much greater is that truth for the biblical Christian? I began to evaluate the "why" of every purchase or pursuit. Was it for pleasure, profit, or prestige? Or did it have a value beyond our self-focused desires? Could God use it for His purposes?

In 1994, Kenneth bought a piece of property in the country. I say that Kenneth bought it rather than "we" bought it because I pleaded with and begged him not to purchase it. It had been timbered and looked totally devoid of any redeeming qualities, and frankly, I wanted no more debt. He patiently allowed me to state all the reasons we should not buy this land; then he promised that he would ask his father for advice.

UNWELCOME WISDOM

My father-in-law was one of the few men in my life whom I trusted completely. Surely when he saw this pillaged parcel of land, he would advise against such a foolish purchase.

On a cool Sunday afternoon, we drove Dad up to the top of the hill overlooking "ravaged acres," and he was quiet for a long time. I thought he was deciding how to tell Ken, as gently as he could, that he was a raving maniac even to consider it. Then he looked at Ken and said, "Son, a man without vision will perish."

Oh, great! There will be no turning back now.

The decision to purchase became a wedge in our relationship as Ken spent more and more time and money building and restoring an old log cabin on the property. It became somewhat of an obsession for him. It came to an ugly climax when, three years into the project, I accused Ken of building a shrine to himself. In his anger, he released the entire project to me, saying I could complete it, abandon it, or sell it. He was done with it!

I felt victorious. I would call a realtor in the morning. But I could not find peace with that decision. I had been in pursuit of God for several years by then, so I decided I should seek His counsel, but I assumed He would want us to get rid of this financial burden.

I walked around the property, praying for God's direction. I had an overwhelming sense that I should not sell it. I was confused. It seemed like such an easy solution to unload this burden. I walked through each unfinished room, asking God to give me a vision for what this place could become. His answer: a healing place, a refuge, a sanctuary.

I began to pray for His anointing on the property. I prayed that relationships would be restored here, that wounded or worn out pastors and missionaries could find refuge here.

So we finished the project. We did so together, Ken and I. And we were able to sell some other investments to pay off the cabin property, making it less of a burden for me personally. The cabin truly has become a place of healing and restoration for families, pastors, and missionaries. It also has been used as a retreat center for the staffs of churches and Christian non-profits for prayer and planning. For several years, my sister-in-law has come with the women from her sexual abuse support group. The stories of emotional and spiritual breakthroughs delight my soul and remind me that we are blessed to be a blessing.

Thank You, Lord, for not allowing me to have what I wanted. My vision was so shortsighted. I learned that we must be careful not to presume we know God's plan but must diligently seek His path.

Currently we are continuing the quest for simplicity and are directing more and more of our resources toward building God's kingdom, both at home in the US, and overseas. Nothing brings greater joy than surrendering our shortsighted, earthly desires to the eternal purposes of our Lord and King.

Doing It My Way

~∰◯

WHILE I WAS still in counseling and the Lord was softening my heart, I was forced to confront another lingering issue, a matter of the will. Since I had been deeply wounded by abandonment as a child and young adult, being married to a workaholic was a monumental struggle. It didn't seem to be an issue when we were first married, but as Ken's practice grew, the hours away from home gradually increased until he was working fourteen to sixteen hours a day. He also volunteered to serve on a variety of medical committees and boards, so even when he was at home, he never seemed to be present. His mind always seemed to be elsewhere.

A MARRIAGE IN PERIL

Resentment began to mount, very slowly at first, but over time, it began to erode the foundation of our marriage. Remember, I didn't trust men. So I found myself, sometimes late in the evening, driving by the hospital to see if his car was really in the doctors' parking lot. It always was. It wasn't a mistress this time but a passion of a different variety. The feeling of abandonment, however, was much the same as I had experienced earlier in my life.

It all came to a crisis one evening about fifteen years into our marriage. I had asked Ken to be sure he was not on call one particular evening because I wanted him to attend an event with me. I gave him six weeks notice and reminded him weekly after that.

On the day of the event, at 4:30 in the afternoon, he called to say he would be tied up in the operating room and would not be able to join me. The hurt was deep and the rage explosive. I said that I knew he was not on call and he could let his partner handle whatever came up. He said he felt personally responsible for this patient.

My only words to him were, "You always have to be the hero, don't you? A hero to everyone but your family!" And I hung up the phone. That was it for me. I wanted out of my marriage.

I grabbed the car keys and my Bible and drove to our cabin to calm my anger and finalize my plans for walking out of my marriage. I always had known it couldn't last forever. I sat on the porch swing for hours, crying, praying, and searching Scripture to find a way to justify a divorce. "Lord, this is too much! I can't do this again. My father abandoned us for alcohol, my first husband for another woman, now Ken has abandoned us for his career. I might as well be single. It hurts less."

I was searching the psalms when I came upon Psalm 118:8: "It is better to take refuge in the Lord than to trust in man." I thought, *See, there it is. Even the Bible says you can't trust men.* But the Holy Spirit would not let me linger with such a distorted interpretation for very long. He drew my focus to the phrase, "take refuge in the Lord." Take refuge in the Lord!

I said, "OK, Lord, what are You trying to show me?"

I spent hours wrestling with the Holy Spirit. I didn't want a new understanding; I just wanted out of my marriage. But in the end, the Holy Spirit won. I began to settle down and seek His comfort, His wisdom, and His way. I began to understand a profound truth that would forever change the way I lived and loved. You see, I always had loved others to fill my own void. Make me feel secure, make me feel precious, make me feel worthy, and I will love you. It was a self-focused, conditional love. It was puny and pathetic.

That evening I fully received Christ's unconditional love. I was "filled to the measure of all the fullness of Christ." I sensed a healing, a restoring, and a comfort that I never had known. I began to understand unconditional love. It cannot be earned. It is a gift given. I believe the human heart cannot love unconditionally unless it has received Christ's love—not only to the brim, but also to overflowing. A love that declares, "I love you, period!" Not, "I love you because . . . " or, "I'll love you if . . . ."

Lord, thank You! Thank You! Thank You! This gift is beyond wonderful and words are inadequate to express my gratitude. You are awesome, amazing, Almighty God!

I went home changed—calm, joy-filled, recommitted to an authentic Christian marriage, and surrendered to the will of God. Kenneth began to change as well. As the pressure to fill the void in my wounded heart eased, and as I learned to love him unconditionally, he began to eliminate some of his outside commitments. He eventually joined a larger practice, which decreased his stress load and provided more vacation time. We began to have fun together again. We recently celebrated our thirtieth anniversary. To God be the glory!

Chapter 11

Who, Me?

IT WAS JANUARY, 2001, and Kenneth and I were leaving town in a few days for a medical conference in Puerto Rico. I dropped by the church to speak to our Associate Pastor, Steve. I had heard that the Director of Women's ministry was stepping down because of family issues and no one was lining up to take her place. Since I had been in leadership positions professionally, I simply offered to act as an interim until God called someone so we wouldn't have to shut down the ministry.

Pastor Steve asked, "So is this ministry by default?"

My answer was a bewildered, "Yes, I guess you could call it ministry by default." Then we both laughed, and I left for the airport.

The next day, Ken attended a meeting that did not pertain to my specialty, so I sat under a palm tree near the beach with my Bible and journal, hoping to write a vision for my life for the next year. After a lingering, intimate time of prayer, I began to formulate a vision of what I hoped to accomplish in my personal and professional life. As I began to write, the phrase, "Not by default, but by design," crept into my thoughts. I dismissed it. But like an advertising jingle that worms its way into your mind, this phrase would not go away. All through the morning it poked and penetrated. So I wrote it in the margin of my journal. It wasn't until I penned the words that I made the connection to my conversation with Pastor Steve. *No! Surely this can't be referring to women's ministry. No, surely not. I am an ex-feminist, remember? Lord, You can't be serious! I don't even like women. They're shallow, petty, and backbiting!*

But over the next three days, all doubt left my mind. God was calling *me* into women's ministry. *This has to be some kind of joke. God, You really must have a sense of humor. But really, I don't want to do this. Lord, I really,* really *don't want to do this!*

By the time we arrived back in the US, I had surrendered, saying, "OK, Lord, not my will, but Yours be done. I don't know how I am going to pull this off, but I am willing to learn whatever it is You are trying to teach me. But, please, teach it to me fast so I can move on to something that would be a better fit for me, OK?"

I served as Director of Women's Ministry for five years and met some wonderful models of mature Christian femininity. Notice what I said? Femininity—something I had worked most of my adult life to overcome. I never had wanted to be associated with the soft and vulnerable traits of women, which I considered a setup for betrayal. But here I was, not only being loved by them but also wanting to learn from them. I wanted to understand their strength, their confidence, and their comfort in the knowledge that they served a sovereign God. They lived beyond fear of betrayal. So this is what a godly woman looks like! For the first time in my life, I found peace and comfort in my own femininity.

MINISTERING TO ONE WOMAN

I had been serving as the women's ministry director for several years and loving it when I got a call from the daughter of my mother's new husband. She informed me that her father had had a heart attack and was in the hospital and that my mother was unable to take care of herself. I thought that was strange. She had seemed fine the last time I saw her a few months earlier.

I called my sister in Florida, and we traveled to Michigan together to check on Mom. It became obvious, very quickly, that Mom was beyond the early stages of Alzheimer's. Apparently, her husband had been caring for her and covering for her. We arranged for additional personal services for her, took away her car, and assumed responsibility for her finances.

We returned home thinking she was safe and secure. Days later, she had a stroke. I returned to Michigan, and after her release from rehabilitation, I moved her to North Carolina with me. I thought it would be temporary. But her husband died, and she had no one left in Michigan to care for her. All her children now lived out of state.

"Lord, I can do this, I think," I prayed. But the days dragged into weeks and the weeks into months, and I could do nothing else but care for her. She had a panic attack each time I went to the mailbox at the curb because she couldn't see me. Eventually, Kenneth and I realized we would need to find a facility for her, but Alzheimer's beds were limited and the waiting lists long.

I began to whine and complain to God. "Lord, I thought You called me into women's ministry, and here I am locked away with my mother, who barely knows me. I have no time for anything but her care. And You know me. Patience is not one of my gifts."

But only silence answered me. I learned to feed her, dress her, wipe her bottom, and bathe her. Rather humbling, I must admit. I was learning more about patience than I wanted to know. In the late afternoons, we sat together, and I sang hymns to her. Incredibly, she could mouth every word. I remember watching her face as her lips formed the words of "Amazing Grace."

She seemed so childlike, so precious, and so much at peace. The lump in my throat abruptly ended my singing, but she sang on, not that anyone but the Lord could hear. I finally said, "OK, Lord, I am sorry for all my whining and complaining. If this is what You have for me to do, I will give up everything else and care for her. Not my will, but Yours be done." Then there was peace in surrender.

Within the next week, we got a call that there was an opening in the Alzheimer's unit in the Christian nursing home five minutes from our home. We visited and knew it was the perfect place for Mother. And it was the perfect answer to prayer for me. I could return to the ministry that I knew was God's call for me and remain intimately involved in my mother's care until her death four years later.

In retrospect, I believe it was God's will for me to bond emotionally with my mother and to develop the spiritual fruit of patience, kindness, goodness, faithfulness, and gentleness. More importantly, I needed to acknowledge that I am not in charge. I am simply His humble servant, surrendering to His assignments on His timeline, for His purpose, and for His glory.

I had found peace in the crucified life!

Reflecting on Your Own Story

WHY GO BACK and ponder the past? Because if we don't, we may fail to see what God is doing in us and through us. Christian counselor and author Dr. Dan Allender writes in *To Be Told*, "Most people don't know how to read their life in a way that reveals their story. They miss the deeper meaning in their life, and they have little sense of how God has written their story to reveal himself and his own story."[1]

He goes on to say:

> Most of us have spent more time studying a map to avoid getting lost on a trip than we have studying our life so we'll know how to proceed into the future . . . . Our own life is the thing that most influences and shapes our outlook, our tendencies, our choices, and our decisions. It is the force that orients us toward the future, and yet we don't give it a second thought, much less a careful examination. It's time to listen to our own story.[2]

So that is exactly what I challenge you to do—write your story. You do not have to be a gifted writer or a philosophical thinker. Just ask the Lord to guide you, to give you wisdom, discernment, and a willingness to face the past in the light of truth. If you are not a woman who enjoys writing, this task may seem a bit overwhelming, but I believe it will be worth your effort.

Here is a random list of questions that may "jumpstart" your memory, but please do not limit your story to simply answering these questions. This is not an assignment but an important process of reflection.

➤ Who were the important people in your life?
➤ Who left a lasting impact?

- ➢ What were the crisis moments?
- ➢ What caused you the greatest pain?
- ➢ What were your passions?
- ➢ What brought you the greatest joy?
- ➢ When did you feel most secure?
- ➢ When did you feel most alone?
- ➢ Where or when did God begin to reveal Himself?
- ➢ Were there times when you looked for Him but He was silent or seemed absent?
- ➢ What are some things you work very hard to hide?
- ➢ Whose love do you work the hardest to earn?
- ➢ Whose criticism hurts the most?
- ➢ Whom do you most need to impress?
- ➢ What makes you feel burdened?
- ➢ What events bring you the greatest pleasure to remember?
- ➢ What were you doing when you felt at your very best?
- ➢ When are you most at rest?
- ➢ With whom do you feel most real?
- ➢ What were some opportunities that changed the course of your life?
- ➢ What were some of your greatest disappointments?
- ➢ What doubts have caused you to struggle in your faith?
- ➢ What events or life episodes have brought you closer to God?

May I suggest a two-step approach?

Using a stack of three-by-five cards, write each memory on its own card with an approximate date in one of the upper corners. Be very brief in this phase. Then arrange the cards in chronological order. Lay them out vertically or horizontally, like a timeline of your life. This way, you can get the big picture and be sure you have not missed something important.

Begin with the first card, and start writing your story. Recall the sights, sounds, smells, and especially the feelings. Do not deny the pain, do not soften the edges of shame or humiliation, and do not worry that someone will read your story. The choice to share it is entirely yours.

Please do not rush this part of the process. There is no need to set a deadline. If you have established a regular weekly meeting time with a friend or small group, continue to meet for prayer and encouragement. Discuss the process. When you have finished compiling your story cards, even if you have not written the narrative, you are ready to begin the process of "taking off your old self," which we will focus on in Part Two.

L. E. Maxwell, in his book *Born Crucified*, writes, "I must choose whether I will be dominated by the hideous monster self or by Christ. The life that 'Christ lives in me' must have a happy 'yet not I' at its very heart. How can I have the benefits of Christ's death while I still want my own way? Self must be dethroned. I am indeed promised newness of life, but only on the basis that I put off the old self."[3]

So let's begin. In Part Two, we will walk together through the process of surrendering your worldview, wounds, wants, and will so you can experience the "promised newness of life." I encourage you to begin with a time of prayer, asking for wisdom and revelation.

Part Two

Taking off the Old Self

After we are converted to Christ, we must be converted to his cross. The conversion to the cross is an ongoing process that involves a series of deaths: death to experiencing life on our own terms, death to our quest for comfort and happiness, death to our own dreams, and death to autonomy and independence. Death is the only way to resurrection, and none of these deaths is bigger than God.

—Kenneth Boa[1]

Chapter 13

Clarifying Your Worldview

IT IS 2011, and we are living in a post-Christian culture in North America. Like the nation of Israel in the Old Testament, we have lost our moral anchor. Intolerance for biblical Christianity is on the rise. The battle rages for the mind and heart of our relatively young nation. What will we look like twenty years from now? Will we still have our freedom to worship openly, proclaim God's truth publically, and educate our children biblically?

It is a challenging time for Christian women. So let's look at a few fundamental changes taking place in the culture that have impacted our worldview—not only in the culture but also, sadly, in the church.

So what is a *worldview* exactly? After looking at many definitions from the simplest to the most sophisticated, I'd like to summarize and suggest that your worldview is the sum total of your beliefs, assumptions, expectations, convictions, and values that determine how you answer the fundamental questions of life, such as:

- Where did I come from?
- Why am I here?
- How do I fit in the world around me?
- What is truth?
- What is the source for moral values?
- Is there any ultimate authority?
- Is there hope for the future?
- What happens after death?

Of course, this list can go on and on, but you get the picture.

I am far from an expert on this topic, but I think it is important to look at a few of the factors that have had a significant influence on our contemporary western culture and the North American church.

SECULAR HUMANISM

In 2000, Tim LaHaye wrote in his book *Mind Siege*:

> It is no overstatement to declare that most of today's evils can be traced to Secular Humanism, which already has taken over our government, the United Nations, education, television, and most of the other power centers of life . . . . Secularists scorn creationism, design in nature, man in the image of God, the Fall, traditional or biblical morality, the natural family of father and mother, and the religious and political faith of the majority of America's Founding Fathers.[1]

LaHaye summarized some of the core beliefs of humanism:[2]

1. Atheism: Humanists say there is insufficient evidence to support a belief in a supernatural. They begin with man, not God, and see no divine purpose for the human race. They value knowledge and self-sufficiency and believe that humans are responsible for themselves.
2. Evolution: Humanists believe that man has emerged as the result of a continuous, natural evolutionary process.
3. Amorality: Humanists believe that ethics stem from human need and interest and that they are situational. In other words, there are no moral absolutes. They also believe that "puritanical cultures" and "orthodox religions" have suppressed sexual conduct, and they are calling for sexual liberation.
4. Autonomous, self-centered man: Humanists "strive for the good life, here and now. . . . Reason and intelligence are the most effective instruments that humankind possesses. . . . Women should have the right to their own bodies. This includes reproductive freedom, voluntary contraception, and abortion."
5. Socialistic one-world government: Humanists "deplore the division of humankind on nationalistic grounds. . . . The world needs at some point in the future to establish an effective World Parliament. . . . We recommend an international system of taxation."

So let me summarize in my own words: no God, no absolute truth, no moral standards, no purpose, no plan, no hope. Does that sound like something most people are longing for? And yet, we are reluctant to share our truth for fear of being rejected. Interesting to think about.

As I look back over my own journey, I realize that I never would have called myself a secular humanist, but far too many of my beliefs and behaviors were consistent with this worldview. Before my personal encounter with Christ:

- I wanted no moral authority over my life.
- I wanted sexual freedom and easily would have chosen abortion if my birth control had failed.
- I was striving for the "good life" with little or no thought of life after death.
- I was university educated and placed a very high value on intellect and personal achievement.
- Though I wasn't a professed atheist, my lifestyle reflected no fear of God.

NEW AGE SPIRITUALITY

Let's take a look at another powerful influence in our culture: New Age spirituality. The Bible talks about this kind of influence in 2 Timothy 4:3: "For the time will come when men will not put up with sound doctrine. Instead, to suit their own desires, they will gather around them a great number of teachers to say what their itching ears want to hear."

Dr. David Jeremiah provides a few fundamental precepts of New Age spirituality in his book *Invasion of Other Gods*:

1. The universality of God suggests "there is no real distinction between humankind and nature; matter, time, and space are unreal myths that must be eliminated. . . . Instead of an omnipotent God, there is a cosmic force of the universe . . . God is in everything, so whatever exists . . . is part of God."[3]
2. There is no difference between good and bad. "If everything is God, then what is bad is God and what is good is God, and there really isn't any distinction."[4]
3. The unity of the cosmos "teaches that all reality, including God, humankind, the created universe, earth, time, space, and energy, are all connected in divine consciousness."[5]
4. The finality of experience suggests that "you validate what you believe according to your experience."[6] No fundamental truth, just your own experience.
5. Belief in higher consciousness says that in order to be spiritual "you must get out of your body, out of your mind, so that you can ascend to the next level, to your higher consciousness. With trances, mediums, and spirit guides, you can attain your higher consciousness and be absorbed into the universe."[7]
6. Intercession of higher spirits calls upon the services of psychics or mediums to contact the spiritual realm.[8]

The foundation of New Age spirituality is based on Eastern religions mixed with occult practices that are forbidden by Scripture. How has this movement infiltrated the Christian church? Let's look at two of the resources being used in churches today that promise physical, mental, and spiritual health, as well as material prosperity.

A COURSE IN MIRACLES

In 1965, psychologist, educator, and self-proclaimed atheist Dr. Helen Schucman was bothered by and intrigued with an "inner voice" that commanded her to write all that she heard. She acted as a "channeler" for this inner voice over a period of seven years and completed 1,200 pages of her writings in 1972.[9]

Though her material contains many references to God, Christ, and the Holy Spirit, the *Encyclopedia of New Age Beliefs*, by John Ankerberg and John Weldon, tells us, "These materials comprise occult revelations, and were produced by means that the Bible forbids (Deut. 18:9–12)."[10]

To see if this movement is still having an impact, I did a little Internet search and found that it is very much alive and well. Here is an excerpt from the website of the Foundations for a Course in Miracles.

> The Workbook includes 365 lessons, one for each day of the year.
>
> Some of the ideas the workbook presents you will find hard to believe, and others may seem to be quite startling. This does not matter. You are merely asked to apply the ideas as you are directed to do. You are not asked to judge them at all. You are asked only to use them. It is their use that will give them meaning to you, and will show you that they are true.
>
> Remember only this; you need not believe the ideas, you need not accept them, and you need not even welcome them. Some of them you may actively resist. None of this will matter, or decrease their efficacy. But do not allow yourself to make exceptions in applying the ideas the workbook contains, and whatever your reactions to the ideas may be, use them. Nothing more than that is required.

Please tell me that frightens you! Do not think, do not judge for yourself, do not resist; simply apply the ideas without exception. Followers learn that they are not separate from God, as the Bible proclaims, but are one in essence with Him, reflecting the new age belief that "man is inwardly divine. Therefore, being one essence with God, he powerfully molds and creates his own reality. . . . Man's greatest problem, therefore, is not sin but ignorance. So he must learn how to manipulate his consciousness in order to perceive 'true' reality and mold it according to his wishes."[11] You can find *A Course in Miracles* taught at many mainline churches, particularly in urban settings.

THE SECRET

A second resource that has found its way into the church is a more recent and *very* widely read publication, which was passionately promoted by one of the most influential American daytime talk show hosts. As I've traveled internationally, I have seen this book in many languages in prominent displays in airports and bookstores. It is *The Secret* by Rhonda Byrne. Here are a few excerpts:

> You are the most powerful magnet in the Universe! You contain a magnetic power within you that is more powerful than anything in this world, and this unfathomable magnetic power is emitted through your thoughts.[12]
>
> Your thoughts become things! Say this over and over to yourself and let it seep into your consciousness and your awareness. Your thoughts become things.[13]
>
> As you think, those thoughts are sent out into the Universe, and they genetically attract all *like* things that are on the same frequency. Everything sent out returns to the source. And that source is You.[14]
>
> Your transmission creates your life and it creates the world. The frequency you transmit reaches beyond cities, beyond countries, beyond the world. It reverberates throughout the entire Universe.[15]
>
> To attract money, you must focus on wealth . . . . You must focus on the abundance of money to bring that to you . . . . The only reason any person does not have enough money is because they are *blocking* money from coming to them with their thoughts.[16]
>
> Illness cannot exist in a body that has harmonious thoughts. Know there is only perfection, and as you observe perfection you must summon that to you. Imperfect thoughts are the cause of all humanity's ills, including disease, poverty, and unhappiness.[17]

Have you read this book? Have you been appalled by the blasphemous statements? Have you participated in a study of this book at your church?

My sister called one day last year and wanted to know what I thought about *The Secret* because several women in her Christian women's group wanted to study it. Even after she told them the truth of what she had discovered, she could not dissuade them. The pastor did not have a problem with the study. Since there were several biblical passages in the book, "it must be OK." When I think of that church, it reminds me of the verse of Scripture that says, "They were like sheep without a shepherd" (Mark 6:34). My sister has since found a new church.

Please don't misunderstand me. I am not trying to suggest that we read nothing but biblically-based materials. I believe it is important for us to understand the culture if we are to be ambassadors for Christ in our communities. But to allow the study of *A Course in Miracles* or *The Secret*, as if they were just another Bible study, is like opening the gates of the sheep pen and letting the wolf in to roam around and whisper lies and half-truths to lure the sheep into complacency before he devours them.

The ultimate battle is, and always has been, a spiritual one. Chip Ingram says, "We are involved in an invisible war, a cosmic conflict that has eternal implications. It is real, it is serious, and it is ultimate in its consequences."[18]

But do not despair! The Lord reminds us in John 16:33 that in Him we can have peace. Even though in this world we will have trouble, we can "take heart" for He has overcome the world!

THE POLITICAL REALM

As I write this manuscript, our country is horribly divided politically, fueling hostility even in the church. If I mention to a small group of people that I am a Christian who believes in the sanctity of life, they might assume that I am a "right-wing" conservative Republican. If I say I have a broken heart for the poor, the illiterate, the imprisoned, and the environment, they might categorize me as a "left-wing" liberal Democrat.

When did biblical truth become the sole domain of a political party? As biblical Christians, we are not of this world (John 15:19). We are expected to keep ourselves from being polluted by the world (James 1:27). We are to stand above the fray. This is not to suggest that we keep silent or stay at home on voting day. It simply means that "we have put our hope in the living God" (1 Tim. 4:10), not in government. We examine the issues against biblical truth, not political affiliation. When we are more closely identified with a political party than as a disciple of Christ, we have lost our firm foundation, to the detriment of our message. That message is simple: "God our Savior wants all men to be saved and to come to a knowledge of the truth. For there is one God and one mediator between God and men, the man Christ Jesus, who gave himself as a ransom for all men . . . (1 Tim. 2:3–6).

RELIGION INSTEAD OF RELATIONSHIP

Sadly, religion itself has negatively influenced a biblical worldview for many Christian women. Churches that lean strongly toward either *license* or *legalism* have distorted biblical truth. Let me give you an example from my own life.

License

I was raised in a church that preached an evangelical message every week, making me believe that the only important thing was praying the "prayer of salvation" and walking to the altar to confess my conversion publicly. I didn't understand that this was the *first* step to faith; I thought it was the *ultimate* step of faith. I was redeemed, forever saved from hell. I no longer needed to listen to the Sunday sermons because I already had bought my ticket to paradise. I never heard a message about holiness and wouldn't have expected it. After all, we are only human.

Our Sunday school classes were generally geared to helping us learn how to evangelize our friends and families. We had lots of Bible verses to memorize, but they always seemed to be about sinners and salvation. So with this as my background, even years later in the midst of my sinful rebellion, I would have told you that I was a "born-again" believer on my way to heaven. My attitude might have been expressed like this, "Sure, I have been a naughty girl, but Daddy loves me anyway." Is there any truth to that statement? Sure! Abba (Daddy) did love me anyway. But let's take a look at several Scripture verses from 1 John:

> If we confess our sins, he is faithful and just to forgive us our sins and purify us from all unrighteousness.
>
> —1 John 1:9

> We know we have come to know him if we obey his commands. The man who says, "I know him," but does not do what he commands is a liar, and the truth is not in him.
>
> —1 John 2:3–4

> Everyone who has hope in him purifies himself, just as he is pure.
>
> —1 John 3:3

> But you know that he appeared so that he might take away our sins. And in him is no sin. No one who lives in him keeps on sinning. No one who continues to sin has either seen him or known him.
>
> —1 John 3:5–6

> No one who is born of God will continue to sin, because God's seed remains in him; he cannot go on sinning, because he has been born of God.
>
> —1 John 3:9

That is truth! So the question is this: Was I saved, or did I live in the deception of a false conversion? I lived in *license*; I "changed the grace of our God into a license for immorality" (Jude 4). I believed it was not possible for a human to live a "holy life," so I wasn't going to burden myself with the effort. After all, I just wanted enough faith to keep me from the fire.

Legalism

When I began my serious quest for truth, we visited, and later joined, a church that had come from the "holiness" tradition. Here I began to recognize something entirely new—women who carried with them the incredible burden of being "holy enough." Neil Anderson, in his book *Breaking the Bondage of Legalism*, suggests that, "As cruel and heartless as physical bondage can be, spiritual bondage is worse . . . where joy is stolen, faith is sometimes killed, and hope is often destroyed."[19]

During my years as Director of Women's Ministry, I heard sad stories of young girls who felt they never could live up to their parents' expectations. Perfectionism seemed to be the goal, and the proof was in the outward appearance of "holiness." They could not wear makeup or jewelry, attend movies or dances, or wear slacks to church. If a girl got pregnant out of wedlock, it brought unbearable shame and rejection.

The degree of guilt these women often carried affected their relationships, first with God, then with everyone else. It destroyed intimacy and authenticity. They had to learn to wear the "mask" if they were to be accepted. Neil Anderson continues, "If you have been trapped in a legalistic system of rigid rules, regulations, and standards, chances are you have grown to mistrust your own God-given discernment. You have relied on others to tell you what is right and wrong."[20]

Anderson offers this definition of legalism:

> Christian legalism is seeking to attain, gain, or maintain acceptance with God, or achieve spiritual growth, through keeping a written or unwritten code or standard of performance . . . Christian legalism is a dead-end street that drains away spiritual vitality, steals our joy, dulls our passion for God, and drives many people into depression.[21]

But there is hope! Through the study of God's Word, illuminated by the Holy Spirit, you can know the truth for yourself.

When Jesus walked the earth, His greatest admonishment and His harshest words were not for the sinful but for the teachers of the law. He said, "Woe to you, teachers of the law and Pharisees, you hypocrites! You are like whitewashed tombs, which look beautiful on the outside but on the inside are full of dead men's bones and everything unclean. In the same way, on the outside you appear to people as righteous but on the inside you are full of hypocrisy and wickedness" (Matt. 23:27–28).

Jesus described the teachers of the law as men who "tie up heavy loads and put them on men's shoulders, but they themselves are not willing to lift a finger to move them" (Matt. 23:4). These heavy loads are in contrast with what He says in Matthew 11: "Come to me, all you who are weary and burdened, and I will give you rest. Take my yoke upon you and learn from me, for I am gentle and humble in heart, and you will find rest for your souls. For my yoke is easy and my burden is light" (Matt. 11:28–30).

As you read that scripture, what feelings does it evoke? Re-read it. Meditate upon it. Is it inviting and comforting? Or does it generate a cynical response because, for you, religion has always carried with it a burden of perfection that never provides rest for the soul? Listen to the words of the apostle Paul:

> You foolish Galatians! Who has bewitched you? Before your very eyes Jesus Christ was clearly portrayed as crucified. I would like to learn just one thing from you: Did you receive the Spirit by observing the law, or by believing what you heard? Are you so foolish? After beginning with the Spirit, are you now trying to attain your goal by human effort?
>
> —Galatians 3:1–3

Whether you have followed the path of license or legalism, the Lord wants to offer you *liberty*.

Liberty

When I was a young girl, prior to my wounding and rebellion, I loved my mother dearly. She was gentle, loving, patient, kind, and uncritical. I never received a harsh spanking, a hateful look, or a caustic remark from her. I *never* doubted her love. I lived in obedience because I would not purposely have done anything to hurt or dishonor her. I was not perfect, of course, but I cannot remember any intentional disobedience. It was simple, unquestioning, childlike love. It never was about trying to earn her love or acceptance.

Jesus said, "I tell you the truth, anyone who will not receive the kingdom of God like a little child will never enter it" (John 10:15). I think He is asking us to love Him with childlike love—to love Him enough to trust Him to know what is best for us and to live in obedience to Him out of that love, not out of fear of punishment. For many of us, our experiences in childhood were more about abuse, abandonment, and betrayal, so trusting is harder and does not come naturally.

Recently, I was sitting in a restaurant, waiting for my husband to join me, and I was captivated by a young father and his baby daughter sitting in a nearby booth. He was fully engaged in the precious moment with her. He maintained eye contact, smiled and cooed, jostled her in the air, and wore a grin of delight as if she were the only child on earth. She laughed, her eyes glued to his, reached up and touched his face, and then leaned into his chest. And she smiled.

It was a private moment, but it warmed my soul. That is what I think of when I hear those words, "Let the little children come to me" (Mark 10:14). This is what I think Jesus is talking about: this childlike faith that finds security, comfort, love, and trust in the Lord. A love so intense that you believe if you had been the only sinner to walk the earth, He would have gone to the cross just for you, to set you free from the law of sin and death; there is no longer any condemnation, only rest for your weary soul. Now *that* is liberty!

George Barna, in his book *Growing True Disciples*, writes, "The Christian church is failing to live up to its promise; we're not even coming close to fulfilling it. . . . Believers are largely indistinguishable from nonbelievers in how they think and live. The church has lost its place at the table of cultural influence. . . . It will take zealots for Christ—individuals who are intractably devoted to knowing, loving, and serving Him with all their heart, mind, strength, and soul—if we are to transform our world."[22]

I want to stake my claim in this culture and in the church as a zealot for Christ! Will you join me? We must begin with a biblical worldview. In his book *Think Biblically*, John MacArthur says, "A truly *Christian* worldview, simply put, is one in which the Word of God, rightly understood, is firmly established as both the foundation and the final authority for everything we hold true."

Action step: Review your life story cards, and identify any areas of your life that have been influenced by competing worldviews or a distorted understanding of the Bible.

Reflection question: Who or what has been the greatest influence in shaping your worldview, either positively or negatively?

Search the Scriptures: For further study, see the list of helpful scriptures in Appendix 4, page 153.

Prayer: Spend time in prayer, reflecting and receiving what the Holy Spirit wants to reveal to you. *Respond in your journal.*

Chapter 14

Healing Our Wounds Starts with Forgiveness

ONE OF THE most difficult barriers to spiritual growth is our tenacious clinging to wounds of the past. Those memories victimize us over and over again. They consume our thoughts, color our outlook, and drain our vitality. We can't move forward in Christ until we make the choice to heal. But how? Not by denying the past, glossing over the pain, or excusing the behavior.

Dan Allender, in *The Wounded Heart*, says, "The answer involves a strategy that seems to intensify the problem: *peer deeply into the wounded heart.* The first great enemy to lasting change is the propensity to turn our eyes away from the wound and pretend things are fine."[1]

That was my strategy. It didn't work for me, and it won't work for you either. I am not a trained counselor, but I know the transforming power of the greatest counselor, the Holy Spirit, Who "will teach you all things" (John 14:26), for He is the "Spirit of truth" (John 15:26). Truth will be a key factor in your healing. As Allender says, "Honesty is the commitment to see reality as it is, without conscious distortion, minimization, or spiritualization. . . . Honesty takes away the need for living a life of lies."[2]

Like I did, you may need the help of a professional Christian counselor to break through to freedom. But I encourage you to begin the process with the Word and the Holy Spirit. I believe there are three areas that can hold you in bondage:

1. Failure to forgive God
2. Failure to forgive those who have wounded you
3. Failure to forgive yourself

Forgiving God

One of the hardest questions to overcome is the gnawing cry, "God, where were you when this was happening to me?" If God is sovereign, then He allowed this to happen. Why? What possible good can come from this? Can you ever trust Him again?

Several years ago, while on vacation, I had the opportunity to talk with a man who seemed to love the Lord, but he could not reconcile that a good God would allow bad things to happen to His children. He had chosen to believe that God created the world and set it in motion but He does not intervene. He merely watches from afar and will judge us in the end. It was the only way he could find peace and put away the gnawing question, "Why, God?" But this view, though somewhat comforting for him, is not biblical. God is not distant, uninvolved, or unavailable. Even a superficial scanning of Scripture will dispel that thought.

> And I will ask the Father, and he will give you another counselor to be with you forever—the Spirit of truth. The world cannot accept him because it neither sees him nor knows him. But you know him, for he lives with you and will be in you.
>
> —John 14:16–17

> Remain in me and I will remain in you. No branch can bear fruit by itself; it must remain in the vine . . . I am the vine; you are the braches. If a man remains in me and I in him, he will bear much fruit; apart from me you can do nothing.
>
> —John 15:4–5

> And surely I am with you always, to the very end of the age.
>
> —Matthew 28:20

Brennan Manning, in *Abba's Child*, writes, "The Christ within who is our hope of glory is not a matter of theological debate or philosophical speculation. He is not a hobby, a part-time project, a good theme for a book, or a last resort when all human effort fails. He is our life, the most real fact about us. He is the power and wisdom of God dwelling within us."[3]

So what do you do with the nagging question, "God, where were you when this was happening to me?" You must make the *choice* to trust His goodness, even though you do not understand. Failure to do this will leave you forever bound by Satan's lies. God is either good or He is not. Dan Allender says, "Those who trust God most are those whose faith permits them to risk wrestling with Him over the deeper questions of life."[4] A. W. Tozer says, "Nothing twists and deforms the soul more than a low or unworthy conception of God."[5]

Pour out your grief and pain to God. Be specific! Verbalize what you think and feel! He already knows anyway. Then seek forgiveness for your resentment and unforgiving spirit. Ask for the peace that passes all understanding, and begin to cultivate an eternal perspective. Our problems and our pain pale in the light of eternity, where they will be remembered no more.

FORGIVING OTHERS

So many scriptures compel us to forgive. Here are just a few:

> For if you forgive men when they sin against you, your heavenly Father will also forgive you. But if you do not forgive men their sins, your Father will not forgive your sins.
>
> —Matthew 6:14–15

> Do not judge, and you will not be judged. Do not condemn, and you will not be condemned. Forgive, and you will be forgiven.
>
> —Luke 6:37

> And when you stand praying, if you hold anything against anyone, forgive him, so that your Father in heaven may forgive your sins.
>
> —Mark 11:25

Yet very few believers actually grieve over their failure to forgive. Instead, we wear our bitterness as a badge of our suffering and wonder why we do not experience the "joy of the Lord." Sadly, we drain the joy of those closest to us as well.

The first step in forgiving others requires a decision, a *choice* to live in obedience. It doesn't matter whether or not he or she deserves to be forgiven. It doesn't matter whether or not you "feel" like forgiving. So how do you go about it? You submit to the process of surrendering the abuse, the abandonment, the betrayal, and the pain and bitterness it caused. Accept the reality that those sins were nailed to the cross with Christ, and trust the Holy Spirit to do a supernatural work in you.

Let me share more of my story: My counselor encouraged me to confront the truth. She asked me to go away for a time of solitude and prayer. I was to write a letter to "little Marie" and identify all the painful episodes of her life, creating a clear picture of the reality she had had to endure. I felt foolish at first, but I wrote and I wept. It was a time to purge and a time to grieve.

Then it was time to pray. My prayer went something like this: "Abba Father, I am overwhelmed with sadness and pain. I have tried to overcome this bitterness, but it continues to eat away at my soul, leaving a gaping hole that nothing can fill. I am exhausted with the effort to keep on 'keeping on.' I know that You expect me to overcome, but I haven't been able to do it. God, I can't survive this disobedience any longer. Will You please take this burden of bitterness from me? I surrender it to You. Crucify it, I pray. I hunger for intimacy with You more than I long to hold on to these wounds. Fill me with Your peace, Lord. I need You so desperately. Amen."

When I finished praying, I was emotionally spent. I went to bed and slept deeply. In the morning, I woke to newness of life, bitterness gone, joy restored, and gratitude overflowing. It was a supernatural work of the Holy Spirit, but I had to make the choice—the choice to surrender my wounds and live in obedience.

FORGIVING YOURSELF

For some believers, the barrier to freedom is a failure to forgive themselves. Steven Olford, in his book *Not I but Christ*, shares a story of a missionary who was expounding on the sixth chapter of Romans, affirming that our old self was crucified with Christ, therefore we can live a new life. He asked if there was someone listening who was haunted by his past and defeated in his witness. Olford records the missionary's words for us:

> Do you know that such introspection is a violation of the principle of grace? God has condemned, crucified, and buried your "old self." What right have you to visit the cemetery of your moral past and dig up the bones? Accept by faith what God has done and trust the Holy Spirit to liberate you to live the resurrection life in Christ.[6]

Wow, how about that for a stunning word picture? How many gravediggers do you know? What about you? Do you make regular trips to the cemetery of the past, replaying the guilt and condemnation? In *The Bondage Breaker*, Neil Anderson writes, "God has done all He needs to do for us to live a victorious life in Christ—now we have to assume our responsibility . . . the responsibility as a believer to repent and believe the truth that will set you free."[7]

In Romans 8:1 we read, "Therefore, there is now no condemnation for those who are in Christ Jesus, because through Christ Jesus the law of the Spirit of life set me free from the law of sin and death."

When we keep coming back to claim our sins, it is as if we are setting our standard higher than that of Christ, declaring that His sacrifice on the cross was not sufficient; it was not "finished." However, He either spoke truth or He didn't. Which is it? When we cling to our sins, we never can experience the depth of love and gratitude that comes from forgiveness.

Several years ago, I was meeting with a young woman to mentor her on a weekly basis. I was getting somewhat frustrated as we kept coming back to the same conversation week after week—the issue of her unworthiness. Finally, I took hold of her hand, looked deeply into her eyes, and said, "Yes, you are unworthy! You are unworthy, inadequate, and incapable of doing anything of significance apart from Christ. That's true of all of us. That's why His grace is so amazing. And it's why we rely so completely on Him. We find our worth only in Him; anything more is arrogance, but anything less is a denial of His sufficiency." We didn't need to have that conversation again!

A. W. Tozer gives insight that drives deep into the soul:

The widest thing in the universe is not space; it is the potential capacity of the human heart. Being made in the image of God, it is capable of almost unlimited extension in all directions. And one of the world's worst tragedies is that we allow our hearts to shrink until there is room in them for little beside ourselves.[8]

God wants to heal and expand your heart, but perhaps it contains too many issues of the past, leaving it protected and protracted so that there is no room for the healing presence of the Holy Spirit. When we spend so much time licking our wounds, we fail to move forward in our pursuit of authentic faith. We can spend years wallowing in self-absorption and miss all the blessings of the new life that God has planned for us. Do not linger there another day!

Action step: Review your life story cards. Select the cards that reveal wounds not yet healed. Ask the Holy Spirit to reveal truth and to minister grace as you process through each one.

Reflection question: On whom have you been "keeping a record of wrongs"?

Search the Scriptures: For further study, see the list of helpful scriptures in Appendix 4, page 153.

Prayer: Spend time in prayer, reflecting and receiving what the Holy Spirit wants to reveal to you. *Respond in your journal.*

Chapter 15

When Our Wants Get in the Way

A FEW YEARS ago, my husband and I were on a medical mission trip to Haiti. We had the opportunity to visit a small, rural church that served the "poorest of the poor." The pastor's sermon was on materialism! I looked around at the tattered congregation and was stunned. I thought that surely this sermon was aimed at us, the wealthy Americans. After the service, I found my way to the pastor and asked about the curious selection of the sermon topic. His response burned into my soul: "It's not what we own that makes us materialistic; it is what we hunger for."

When I was in my early thirties and working for a university medical center, there seemed no end to the things I hungered for—professional recognition, prestige, power, and of course, all the possessions that follow such a focus. I remember sitting at the airport one day as I waited to board a plane for a medical conference. I was dressed in my smart, professional suit; carrying a shiny, new briefcase; and all puffed-up with self-importance. A woman, who appeared to be in her late fifties, kept looking at me with a grin that was unnerving. "Do I know you?" I asked.

"No, but I know you. Let me just say that there will come a time when you will spend the second half of your life getting rid of all the things you spent the first half of your life accumulating."

I thought, *What an eccentric old woman!*

But years later, I am still in the process of "getting rid of" those things that have long ago lost their value, purpose, or pleasure. The things we owned became more and more of a burden, merely excess baggage in the pursuit of authentic faith. Now I hunger only to live in His presence, by His power, and for His purpose and pleasure.

Often in our "pursuit of happiness," we come to believe that these temporal things define the "good life," and even Christians have come to expect them. Luxuries have become necessities, and personal want and global need seem to have no connection.

So what is the biblical truth? Consider these passages:

Do not store up for yourselves treasures on earth, where moth and rust destroy, and where thieves break in and steal. But store up for yourselves treasures in heaven, where neither moth nor rust destroys, and where thieves do not break in or steal; for where your treasure is, there your heart will be also.

—Matthew 6:19–21

And the congregation of those who believed were of one heart and soul; and not one of them claimed that anything belonging to him was his own, but all things were common property to them . . . there was not a needy person among them, for all who were owners of land or houses would sell them and bring the proceeds of the sales and lay them at the apostles' feet, and they would be distributed to each as any had need.

—Acts 4:32, 34–35

But godliness with contentment is great gain. For we brought nothing into the world, and we can take nothing out of it.

—1 Timothy 6:6–7

Kenneth Boa reflects on this issue in his book *Conformed to His Image:*

Most of us don't know precisely what we want, but we are certain we don't have it . . . . The truth is that if we are not satisfied with what we have, we will never be satisfied with what we want. . . . The real issue of contentment is whether it is Christ or ourselves who determine the content (e.g., money, position, family, circumstances) of our lives. When we seek to control the content, we inevitably turn to the criterion of comparison to measure what it should look like. The problem is that comparison is the enemy of contentment—there will always be people who possess a greater quality or quantity of what we think we should have. Because of this, comparison leads to covetousness.[1]

If you are a mother, I'm sure you have struggled with the issue of contentment in your children. How many times have you heard them ask, "Can I, Mom, please?" As women who are growing in our faith, we might be willing to deny ourselves, but it is so much more difficult to deny our children. Satan is very much aware of this struggle! And he will use it to cause dissension and drive wedges in our relationships with our children. It is here where we are most likely to compromise. After all, we want our children to be happy, don't we? But as Christians, is it our biblical mandate to raise *happy* children or *holy* children? This passage answers that question:

Faithfully obey the commands I am giving you today—to love the Lord your God and serve him with all your heart and with all your soul . . . Be careful, or you will be enticed to turn away and worship other gods. . . . Fix these words of mine in your hearts and minds. . . . Teach them to your children, talking about them when you sit at home and when you walk along the road, when you lie down and when you get up.

—Deuteronomy 11:13, 16, 18–19

The cure for an endless list of "wants" is really quite simple. "Seek first his kingdom and his righteousness" (Matt. 6:33). The Greek word for kingdom is *basileia,* and it means "kingship" or "royal rule." It is used more than fifty times in the book of Matthew when referring to the kingdom of God.

In the past, when I thought of the "kingdom of God," I thought of a literal place, like heaven. As I have looked at the Greek meaning, I have come to understand that it is not a place, but a state of His lordship, His sovereign rule over everything. We are merely stewards of what He allows us to manage. Psalm 24:1 reminds us, "The earth is the Lord's and everything in it, the world, and all who live in it." The thought that if we give our tithe of ten percent to the church and a little more towards missions, then the rest is ours to do with as we please, is a distortion of the truth.

When Scripture talks about following "the ways of this world and of the ruler of the kingdom of the air" (Eph. 2:2), it uses the word *exousia* for kingdom, which means authority, power, control, or dominion; in other words, the kingdom of Satan. Our list of wants will reflect either the lordship of Christ and His royal kingdom or the control of Satan and his power over our world.

When I said earlier that the cure is "fairly simple," I did not say that it is easy. It is not a "black or white" issue. Material possessions, in themselves, are neither sinful nor self-indulgent. I confess that they can be burdensome, and they come with added responsibility. The same is true of wealth, talent, education, career, and opportunity. Scripture tells us, "From everyone who has been given much, much will be demanded; and from the one who has been entrusted with much, much more will be asked" (Luke 12:48b).

Will I use these gifts to enhance myself and my family or to advance the kingdom of God? In his book *Freedom of Simplicity*, Richard Foster writes:

We are to discipline ourselves to "seek *first* the Kingdom of God." This focus must take precedence over absolutely everything. We must never allow anything, whether deed or desire, to have that place of central importance. The redistribution of the world's wealth cannot be central, the concern for ecology cannot be central, the desire to get out of the rat race cannot be central, the desire for simplicity itself cannot be central. The moment any of these becomes the focus of our concern, it has become idolatry.[2]

I often have been disturbed by Matthew 19:16–22, in which a rich, young man asks Jesus what good thing he must do to get eternal life. Jesus responds by telling him to obey the commandments, and the young man replies, "All these I have kept."

Then Jesus hits him where it hurts! "Go, sell your possessions and give to the poor, and you will have treasure in heaven. Then come, follow me."

The young man went away sad because he had great wealth.

For many years, I assumed that this was a command to all believers who wanted to follow Christ. The Holy Spirit helped me to see that it was required of this young man because his wealth had become his idol. He desired it above the Lord, and we cannot serve both God and money, or any of the things that money can buy (Matthew 6:24).

When I began to think about the effects of the media in driving our hunger for material things, I realized that materialism, in itself, is not so much a worldview as an outcome of a secular mindset. If there is no God or absolute moral truth, then there is no compelling reason to deny myself anything I desire. If the bumper sticker is true, that at the end of life "the one with the most toys wins," and I never will stand before the King of Kings and Lord of Lords to give an account of my life, then why not pursue pleasure, comfort, convenience, and the latest gadgets?

I am somewhat ashamed to say this, but I admire many secular humanists, who, though deceived, are more true to their belief system than many Christians are. It is the reason we have often been labeled "hypocrites," people who profess to have biblical principles and beliefs but behave otherwise. Ouch!

A. W. Tozer reminds us that:

At the root of all true spiritual growth is a set of right and sanctified desires . . . the desire after God and holiness is back of all real spirituality, and when that desire becomes dominant in the life nothing can prevent us from having what we want . . . . While this longing persists there will be steady growth in grace and a constant progress toward Christlikeness. . . . Unsanctified desire will stop the growth of any Christian life. . . . We must surrender our hearts to God so that we have no unholy desires. . . . To want a thing, or feel that we want it, and then to turn from it because we see that it is contrary to the will of God, is to win a great battle on a field larger than Gettysburg or Bunker Hill. To bring our desires to the cross and allow them to be nailed there with Christ is a good and beautiful thing.[3]

Action step: Here is a list of the many things that women in our contemporary western culture want for themselves and their families. Fill in each circle below that is true for you. If I have left anything off the list, just add it in the blank spaces at the end. Let's be honest here, and then add specifics on the adjoining lines to personalize each item.

○ Larger home _____
○ Healthier marriage _____
○ Happier children _____
○ Better health_____
○ More satisfying care _____
○ Greater income_____
○ Education for my children _____
○ Popularity for my children _____
○ Comfort and convenience _____
○ Enhanced beauty _____
○ Recreation _____
○ Entertainment _____
○ Hobby _____
○ Travel _____
○ Higher education _____
○ Stylish wardrobe_____
○ Fine jewelry _____
○ Dining out more often _____
○ New car _____
○ Vacation home _____
○ Country club membership _____
○ _____
○ _____
○ _____

Reflection question: Which of these can you take into eternity with you?

Search the Scriptures: For further study, see the list of helpful scriptures in Appendix 4, page 153.

Prayer: Spend time in prayer, reflecting and receiving what the Holy Spirit wants to reveal to you. *Respond in your journal.*

Chapter 11

Not My Will but His

ARE YOU A strong-willed type like I am? In the flesh, I am arrogant, controlling, and never wrong. I have an opinion about everything and always feel compelled to share it. I am quick to judge, offer advice, and set myself up as the standard by which everyone else should be compared. Thank God, I have been crucified with Christ! I am no longer bound by that sinful, self-willed nature. I have been set free! We read in Galatians 5:24, "Those who belong to Christ Jesus have crucified the sinful nature. . . ."

I am not suggesting that there is no longer any remnant of the "old nature" in me, but the difference is that the moment it sprouts new growth, the Holy Spirit convicts me and conforms me, as long as I humbly submit to His pruning. The longer I have walked this journey with Christ, the less I have had to bear the painful pruning process. He used to use those *enormous* hedge clippers. Now He carries around a small pair of "snipping shears" to use on me. Let's look at this pruning analogy from Scripture:

> I am the true vine, and my Father is the gardener. He cuts off every branch in me that bears no fruit, while every branch that does bear fruit he prunes so that it will be even more fruitful.
>
> —John 15:1–2

What kind of fruit are we supposed to bear? The Bible gives us the answer:

> The acts of the sinful nature are obvious . . . . But the fruit of the Spirit is love, joy, peace, patience, kindness, goodness, faithfulness, gentleness, and self-control.
>
> —Galatians 5:19, 22–23

When I first began to understand the truth of this passage and compared it to the qualities of my own nature, my fruit basket held a very different kind of harvest. It looked more like this: self-absorption, bitterness, agitation, impatience, brashness, arrogance, impulsiveness, criticism, and manipulation. Not a compelling picture of the "abundant life."

I remember my first experience with landscape pruning. We were preparing to put our home on the market, and the front hedges were so overgrown that buyers would not be able to see the architectural detail of the beautiful bay window in the front of the house. Knowing nothing about pruning, I called a gardener and made arrangements for him to prune while I was at the office. When I drove home after work, I gasped at the sight of what appeared to be a devastated front yard. Not a green leaf was left, and the boxwoods that had been at least six feet tall were now no more than two feet tall. I was furious! He had destroyed the yard!

I stormed into the house to call Ken, only to hear him say, "Don't worry, he knows what he is doing. It will come back better than ever."

I was incredulous. *Wait till he sees it*, I thought. *He has no idea.*

Actually, I was the one with no idea! How was it possible? Weeks later, the growth began—lush, healthy, and contained, no longer a wild thing, overgrown and out of control. To this day, every time I read the pruning passages from John, I am reminded of that visual image that so powerfully symbolizes the transforming work of the Holy Spirit. But it always requires our submission, a surrendering of our will.

Keith Drury, in his book *Holiness for Ordinary People*, describes his decision to surrender:

> One windy March day, I settled the issue of Christ's control of my life and placed my total life in His hands . . . I would no longer run the affairs of my life for my own benefit. . . . I have had a consuming passion to obey Christ. He has become the central force of my life. I have this new thirst for holiness. In a sense, I am now a slave to Jesus Christ . . . I decided at one point to submit to His will in everything for all eternity. The issue is settled. . . . I have decided God is Lord of my life. No matter how I feel, I will obey Him. . . . Holiness is not just a priority for me, it is the central priority of my life around which all other priorities orient.[1]

Does this seem rather radical to you? In truth, it is the result of spiritual growth in the fully surrendered, authentic disciple of Christ. Though it is the Holy Spirit Who is responsible for such transformation, we often obstruct the process. We can delay the journey at any step along the way. God has given us a powerful promise, but He will not hold us prisoners to the process. We maintain our power to choose to submit or resist. It is a matter of the will.

Charles Finney, the famed nineteenth century lawyer turned pastor, said, "When a man adopts the opinion that he cannot stop the work of God in his own soul, nothing can be more perilous. . . . Many people do not seem to realize the nature of the Spirit's operations, the possibility of resisting Him, and the great danger of quenching the light of God in the soul."[2]

I am reminded of these disturbing passages from Scripture:

Not everyone who says to me, "Lord, Lord," will enter the kingdom of heaven, but only he who does the will of my Father who is in heaven.
—Matthew 8:21

It is impossible for those who have been once enlightened, who have tasted the heavenly gift, who have shared in the Holy Spirit, who have tasted the goodness of the Word of God and the powers of the coming age, if they fall away, to be brought back to repentance, because to their loss they are crucifying the Son of God all over again and subjecting him to public disgrace.
—Hebrews 6:4

If we deliberately keep on sinning after we have received the knowledge of the truth, no sacrifice for sins is left, but only a fearful expectation of judgment.
—Hebrews 10:26–27

Kenneth Boa reminds us, "The spiritual life should not be reduced to a sudden experience or series of experiences, as meaningful as these may be. Spirituality also involves a process of transformation in which we are progressively conformed to the image of Christ in our character and our conduct."[3]

Dr. V. Raymond Edman, in his book *They Found the Secret*, identifies six stages of life as we move toward the abundant life in Christ.[4]

1. First there is an *awareness* of our need.
2. Then there is *agony* of soul as we become aware of our own depravity.
3. This is followed by a wholehearted, unreserved *abandonment* to the Savior.
4. Then there must be *appropriation* of the Holy Spirit, or the filling of our lives with the presence of the Lord Jesus.
5. That is followed by *abiding*, which Edman defines as "obedience to His will." This is not a striving or struggling; it is a surrendering.
6. This surrender leads to the "exchanged life" or the "crucified life," a life of *abundance*, where "streams of living water" flow from the Spirit-filled life.

It is here, living the "crucified life," that we "bear much fruit" as we abide in Him. Andrew Murray writes, "The believer can each day be pleasing to God only in that which he does through the power of Christ dwelling in him. The daily inflowing of the life-sap of the Holy Spirit is his only power to bring forth fruit. . . . Believers, meditate on this, until your soul bows to worship in the presence of the mystery of the perfect union between Christ and the believer."[5]

It is here where we can live the uncommon life described by A. W. Tozer:

> He feels supreme love for One whom he has never seen . . . empties himself in order to be full, admits he is wrong so he can be declared right . . . is strongest when he is weakest, richest when he is poorest . . . . He dies so he can live, forsakes in order to have, gives away so he can keep, sees the invisible, hears the inaudible, and knows that which passeth knowledge.[6]

Surrendering our will to the Lord does not mean that we give up the essence of who we are. Though we are made in His image, each of us is unique. We have been given personalities, intellects, creativity, talents, spiritual gifts, and passions, each portraying a piece of the mosaic of our lives. These characteristics remain, and even are enhanced, when we surrender our will. The major issue comes down to this: *Who* will sit on the throne of your life—you or Christ? If you are to continue this pursuit of authentic faith and abundant life, you must surrender your right to rule. You must choose to get up off the throne and invite Him to take His rightful place.

Let me warn you, however. It is not a path of comfort and convenience. He does not promise a life free of suffering. For many of us, our greatest periods of spiritual growth and deeper dependence on God came during times of suffering. But He does promise that His grace is sufficient (2 Cor.12:9). We have the grace of the Lord Jesus, the love of God, and the fellowship of the Holy Spirit (2 Cor. 13:14). It is sufficient indeed!

Action step: Review your life story cards, and identify the times that you were in a "battle of the wills" with the Holy Spirit.

Reflection question: In what ways are you intentional in your pursuit to know the will of God?

Search the Scriptures: For further study, see the list of helpful scriptures in Appendix 4, page 153.

Prayer: Spend time in prayer, reflecting and receiving what the Holy Spirit wants to reveal to you. *Respond in your journal.*

The Crucified Life—A Parable of Living Water

THE GOAL OF this parable is to help illustrate the biblical concept of the crucified life. May it spur you on to a more passionate pursuit of authentic faith.

Child of God: Father, there is so much I don't understand about the Christian life. Just what does it mean to be crucified with Christ? And how does the Holy Spirit work in me?

The Father: My child, I will help you to understand using a simple, practical illustration. I want you to find a clear cylinder and then gather four rocks to fit in the cylinder.

Child: What do I need them for?

Father: Child, must you always have all the answers before you are willing to take the first step of obedience?

Child: Sorry, Father, but where will I find these things?

Father: You want me to make it easy for you, child, but I have given you intellect and ingenuity, and I trust that you can use them to fulfill this simple task.

Sometime later . . .

Child: I'm back, Father. What's next?

Father: Stack the four rocks in the cylinder. The cylinder represents you, and the four rocks represent the self-stuff of your human nature. Now bring the cylinder with you. We are going for a walk along the river.

The child looks forward to this time alone with the Lord.

Father: Let's stop here, where the river is flowing freely. I want you to place your cylinder under that small waterfall. Go ahead and position the cylinder so the water flows to fill the cylinder. It will fill and overflow. Now, this is your life after receiving Christ, the "Living Water." You are now my vessel, allowing the Holy Spirit to flow from you. Do you remember being overcome with joy? You experienced a deep, fundamental change. There was hope and peace. You began to be sensitive to the leading of the Holy Spirit. You had a hunger and thirst to know Me more intimately. Your prayer life was richer, and I allowed you the delight of this new faith, for a while.

Child: Yes, Father, I remember. But it didn't last! How come?

Father: Because I want more for you. I want to take you deeper still. I want to conform you to the image of my Son. But in order to do that, there must be less of you and more of Him. It's time to deal with those rocks. Look at them. What do you see?

Child: They are filling so much of the cylinder that there is not much room for the filling of the water.

Father: Yes, child, the flow of the Spirit is hindered by those rocks. Let's remove the first one, called "worldview." You have been so influenced by the world that you don't even recognize the deception and lies.

Child: Please, Father, give me an example.

Father: I know you will have trouble admitting it to me, but you have begun to wonder if there really is only *one* way to God. You have become confused about the difference between sin and alternative lifestyle choices. You have lost the passion for purity, believing that it is perhaps fanatical and out of step with the reality of your contemporary world.

Child: Father, I am embarrassed and ashamed, but it is true.

Father: I know, my child. That is why you need more of the real truth. If you are willing, reach into the cylinder and remove that first rock, but only if you are truly ready. Because it will mean that from now on your source of truth will be My Holy Scriptures. You will need to filter all of your decisions through that truth, with help from the Holy Spirit, of course. Once you remove that rock, there will be more flow of the Living Water.

Child: I'm ready, Father. Here, take it. It makes life less confusing, doesn't it?

Now more room is available for the filling of the Living Water.

Child: Wow! I feel lighter and more confident, less anxious and more trusting. Why is that?

Father: Because you no longer have to wonder what is true, what is noble, what is right, or what is pure or lovely or admirable. You will know it. I will speak to you through My Word, and My Holy Spirit will confirm it.

Child: Father, as wonderful as this feeling is, I want more of You. What's next?

Father: Removing the next rock will be a painful experience, child. Perhaps you want to wait awhile.

Child: Please, Father, let's keep going. I want all of You.

Father: This second rock is called "wounds," and it represents everything that has caused you pain and shame. It also represents everyone who was part of those episodes in your life. It will require great courage and grace to surrender this one. You and I both know the people who hurt you so deeply. And I know that you have blamed Me at times for allowing those things to happen to you. If you decide to dig this rock out of your life, you must give up thinking of yourself as the victim and must take your stand as a victor. It will require that you forgive.

Child: But, Father, some of those people don't deserve forgiveness, and most of them have never asked for it. Do You expect me to forgive people who haven't even acknowledged what they have done to me?

Father: Yes, child, I do. It is exactly that kind of forgiveness that requires the love and grace that can only come from an intimate relationship with Me. It is a testimony of My power to transform human nature—to do the unbelievable and the irrational. And it is only through forgiveness that you will be free from the bondage of those wounds.

Child: I am afraid that the hardest person to forgive might be myself. Some of the things I have done are so shameful that I would rather leave them buried, and the deeper, the better.

Father: So you are saying that when I sent My Son to the cross to pay the debt for those sins, the price He paid was not enough? Is your standard of holiness superior to Mine?

Child: Oh, no, Father! I would never suggest such a thing.

Father: Then will you accept His payment as sufficient and mark the debt "paid in full"? And will you do the same for those who have wounded you? It will mean that you wipe the slate clean, keeping no record of wrongs.

Child: I don't know if I can.

Father: Are you willing?

Child: I'm not sure.

Father: Are you willing to spend more time in the Word and in prayer, asking for a softening of your heart?

Child: Yes, Father, but please don't leave me.

Father: Never will I leave you or forsake you.

Much later . . .

Child: Father, I am ready. I no longer want to grieve You by my disobedience, and I no longer want to be in bondage to the past. I long for peace. I surrender it all to You. Take it! I can't wait to get rid of it. I want to breathe freely!

She hands Him the rock called "wounds," and immediately she has more of Him, the Living Water.

Father: Well done, child. You will experience a newness of life and health beyond all that you could have asked for or imagined.

She worships Him with new passion and thanksgiving.

Child: Abba, I've never before experienced this peace.

Father: It is the peace that passes all understanding, child. But you are just beginning to probe the depths of wisdom and knowledge. There is more yet to come.

Child: How can that be?

Father: Because My divine power has given you everything you need for life and godliness. It is through that power that you can participate in My divine nature.

Child: But I am only human! How can I participate in Your divine nature?

Father: Through the Holy Spirit, Who has come to live within you. You see, when you accepted My Son's payment for your sins, you were crucified with Him. But that also means you were raised with Him to a new life. The Holy Spirit, Who now lives in you, is the power by which you can live this new life—a holy life, just as I am holy.

Child: Does that mean I will not sin—ever again?

Father: No, but it means that you will not go on sinning intentionally. It is the Holy Spirit's job to convict you right away and make you aware that you have offended Him. It is your job, then, to confess it and turn away from it. Over time, you will become so aware of His leading that you will not intentionally sin.

Child: Wow! I never thought that was possible.

Father: Well, we have a little more work to do. You see that next rock? It is called "wants."

Child: Does it represent that new car I was looking at last week?

Father: Oh, it symbolizes so much more than just that car. It represents everything that you want more than you want Me or what I want for you.

Child: Like what?

Father: That promotion and pay raise you applied for yesterday. It will require you to work on Sundays. You have been so blessed by the environment of worship in your new church, and you have spoken so passionately about serving in the children's ministry. You never talked to Me before you decided to pursue this change.

Child: (embarrassed) I guess I knew what You would say, so I didn't ask. I'm sure You would rather I be at the church, but I need the pay raise to be able to buy the car.

Father: It also will require that you take out a loan. Do you remember the bondage of debt you had in the past?

Child: Yes, but I have more self-control now.

Father: I want you to be controlled by My Spirit. I want you to be a faithful steward of all I have given you—not just your income, but also your time, your talents, and your spiritual gifts. I have a plan for you, child, for life abundant. But it cannot be measured by the things of this world. Remember, you are no longer of this world. I have chosen you out of the world.

Child: Father, I want nothing more than I want to love You and please You.

Father: The more time you spend with Me, in My Word and in prayer, the more you will want what I want. Nothing can satisfy your soul like intimacy with Me. When you find yourself hungering for the things of this world, it is probably an indication that you have become distracted and have neglected our time together. As you abide in Me, you will be refreshed and renewed.

Child: I want that, Father. Please take this rock from me. It feels so heavy and burdensome. I want nothing to come before You.

Father: You must realize that this is not a one-time surrender. When you hand Me that rock called "wants," it means that you are giving up your right to choose what you want. All major decisions will be bathed in prayer, seeking the Holy Spirit's guidance. Are you sure you are ready?

Child: That is what You want for me, isn't it?

Father: Yes.

Child: Then I am ready. But what do I do about a new car? Mine is beyond repair.

Father: Trust me.

After a short hesitation, she hands Him the rock called "wants."

Child: I need to learn a lot about trust.

Father: It will come as I prove My faithfulness. I love you and want only what is best for you, not only in this life but also for all eternity. You will not always understand those things I allow to come into your life. But you can trust my goodness.

Child: I want that, Father.

Father: Now that you have gotten rid of that heavy rock, there is so much more room for Living Water, and notice how much less turbulence there is.

Child: Father, I have never felt more content. I feel so much lighter, as if the weight of that rock literally had been on my shoulders.

Father: Not on your shoulders, child. It was crowding your soul.

Child: Father, You are more than sufficient for me. What trinket could possibly compare with You?

Father: My love and grace will always be sufficient, My child.

A time of joy and peace in fellowship with the Holy Spirit follows. Then, as time passes . . .

Father: Child, what pleasure you have brought Me as you have learned to be sensitive to the Holy Spirit. I sense a sincere longing to do what is right, but you are in a battle with the flesh, My child.

Child: What do You mean, Father?

Father: You pride yourself in being self-sufficient; you rarely think you need Me anymore. You make your plans and then carry them out under your own power. You are quick to give advice to others and offer solutions to problems that are none of your concern.

Child: I just thought I was being helpful.

Father: I wish that were your motive.

Child: What do You mean?

Father: Lately you have been critical of others, judging their spiritual maturity and comparing them to yourself. I see evidence of self-righteousness, a bit of pride, and an attempt to assume the role of the Holy Spirit in the lives of others.

Child: But You called me to a life of holiness. That's what I'm trying to live up to.

Father: I called you to a life that is lived in the power of the Holy Spirit. Apart from Me, you can do nothing. You are moving dangerously close to the attitude of the Pharisees. I will not tolerate arrogance.

Child: Father, You're frightening me.

Father: The fear of the Lord is the beginning of wisdom, child.

Child: I do want to be in Your will, Father, but I'm not sure what You want.

Father: Let's return to the cylinder. You see that last rock? It's called "will." It is time for you to surrender it to Me. You are not your own. You have been bought at a great price. You are My child, but you are also My servant and My ambassador. You must represent Me authentically. You can only do that when you are living in My will, not yours.

Child: But, Father, if I give up my will, there will be nothing left of me!

Father: Giving up your will, child, is more like determining who sits on the throne of your life; do you or do I? But you have been given the power to choose this path or not.

Child: Father, please help me to understand. When I give up my will, do I give up everything that makes me unique?

Father: Not at all, child. I knit you together in your mother's womb, and you are fearfully and wonderfully made. I have gifted you with unique personality, intellect, talents, creativity, and passions. I've also have given you spiritual gifts that you have yet to develop fully. You will always have opportunities to express your uniqueness. The difference is that you will use them for My glory and not your own.

Child: I have been so foolish, Father. Please take this "will" from me.

She quickly hands over the rock, as if it were lethal.

Father: Now you have an unobstructed flow of Living Water from deep within you—the promised Holy Spirit—blessing those around you and producing fruit in abundance.

Child: Father, it is beyond words! I am filled to the measure of all the fullness of Christ. And it is more than I could have ever hoped for or imagined; my weakness for His strength, my depravity for His divinity, my poverty for His provision, my arrogance for His humility, my wounds for His healing, and my death for His life.

Father: Now, My child, you have been crucified with Christ, and you no longer live, but Christ lives in you. As a memorial marker of this journey, I have a death certificate for you to sign and keep in your Bible. It will be a daily reminder of your commitment to keep the Holy Spirit flowing from deep within you as you represent My Son in this parched and barren land.

Search the Scriptures: For further study, see the list of helpful scriptures in Appendix 4, page 153.

See page 155 for the Certificate of Death.

Part Three

Putting on the New Self

This is godliness: The more you possess God, the more you are made like Him. But it must be a godliness that has grown from within you. If godliness is not from deep within you, it is only a mask. The mere outward appearance of godliness is as changeable as a garment. But when godliness is produced in you from the life that is deep within you—then that godliness is real, lasting, and the genuine essence of the Lord.[1]

—Jeanne Guyon, a seventeenth-century French saint

Chapter 18

Building a Solid Foundation on the Word

ANYONE WHO KNOWS me well knows *not* to give me a live plant as a gift. It will whither and die very quickly in my care. My mother-in-law, on the other hand, can keep a poinsettia alive through Easter, and the ferns on her porch look like they came straight from the Garden of Eden.

What is the difference? She really nurtures those plants. First of all, she values them, so she waters them, feeds them, picks off the dead foliage, and generally does whatever it takes to make them lush and healthy. Now it's not that I don't value the gift; it's just that I get busy with life and never think about it. If I am honest, I guess I don't value it enough to expend the time, energy, and focus that it takes. So my plants wither and die. What a great word picture for the spiritual life!

In Part Two, you surrendered significant segments of your self-life to God; you have become less so He can become more. It's now time to look at those things you can do to nurture the Spirit within—to commit the time, energy, and focus to establish habits in pursuit of holiness. Failure to be diligent in this area will result in a dry and drooping spiritual life, one that bears little or no fruit. The classic Christian literature might refer to these things as spiritual disciplines. I prefer to call them "habits in pursuit of holiness."

Keith Drury, author of *Holiness for Ordinary People*, writes:

Holiness is loving God with all my heart, mind, soul, and strength, and loving my neighbor as myself. Simply put, holiness is Christ-likeness. Holiness is not an "it" as in "have you got it?" It is *Him* I need. In Him I find purity, power, and obedience . . . it is more than some unreal, far-off, unreachable goal. It is an attainable, present-day experience. It may not be common. Holy living may not be average. But it is possible.[1]

So how do we nurture this budding holiness and live a life of authentic faith? Let's begin by nurturing our relationship with Christ so we can represent Him authentically in a world so desperate for hope and healing. We will be increasingly conformed to His image as we engage in the *Word*, *prayer*, *worship*, and *service*. Let's take a deeper look at these "habits."

IN THE WORD

In years past, before I began my quest for a deep and intimate relationship with Christ, I read my Bible more as a religious requirement than as a lover anticipating a new message from her beloved. How passionate a lover would I be if those letters (or for you younger women, the text messages) remained unopened? How tragic it would be to miss those words of love, comfort, encouragement, instruction, and correction. What would happen to our relationship? How well would I know him? How likely would I be to continue feeling a deep, intense desire for intimacy?

Think about that dusty, unopened Bible on my bedside table of years ago, often covered up by self-help books and travel magazines. Howard Hendricks says, "Dusty Bibles always lead to dirty lives. In fact, you are either in the Word and the Word is conforming you to the image of Christ, or you are in the world and the world is squeezing you into its mold."[2]

THE GIFT OF CHOICE

Before you can begin a serious study of the Word, you must understand the precious and powerful gift you have been given—the gift of choice. The most important factor in your pursuit of authentic faith will be your choice to believe that the Bible is the divinely inspired Word of God, the source of absolute truth. We read in 2 Timothy 3:16–17, "All scripture is God-breathed and is useful for teaching, rebuking, correcting and training in righteousness, so that the man of God may be thoroughly equipped for every good work."

Popular Bible teacher John MacArthur tells us that the Word of God is:

- Infallible in total.
- Inerrant in its parts.
- Complete, so we need not add or subtract.
- Authoritative, so it is truth that demands our obedience.
- Sufficient to meet our every need.
- Effective to do what it says it will do.
- Determinative, because your response to it will determine your destiny.[3]

According to George Barna's research, less than half of all born-again adults believe that there is absolute moral truth.[4] Barna writes: "Our country is a nation immersed in moral anarchy because Americans have abandoned our historic acceptance of the moral virtues and absolutes emanating from the Bible. These days we are more likely to reject moral truth in favor of relativism, opening the floodgates for a top-to-bottom redefinition of our most important values, attitudes, and behaviors."[5]

In *Why I am a Christian*, Paul Hoffman writes, "It all comes down to this. If the Bible is not reliable, then Christianity is a hoax . . . ."[6]

Once you choose to believe that the Bible is true, then you can accept what the Bible says about Christ and what He has said about Himself:

For God did not send his Son into the world to condemn the world, but to save the world through him. Whoever believes in him is not condemned, but whoever does not believe stands condemned already because he has not believed in the name of God's one and only Son.

—John 3:17–18

Whoever believes in the Son has eternal life, but whoever rejects the Son will not see life, for God's wrath remains on him.

—John 3:36

I told you that you would die in your sins: if you do not believe that I am the one I claim to be, you will indeed die in your sins.

—John 8:24

Jesus answered, "I am the way, the truth, and the life. No one comes to the Father except through me."

—John 14:6

Don't you believe that I am in the Father, and the Father is in me? The words I say to you are not my own. Rather, it is the Father, living in me, who is doing his work.

—John 14:10

I have told you these things, so that in me you may have peace. In this world you will have trouble. But take heart! I have overcome the world.

—John 16:33

Belief will build a solid foundation for faith, but it will not sustain your faith, for "even the demons believe" (James 2:19). You must come to *know* Christ, and in that "knowing," you must come to *love* Him. It is love that will keep you hungry and thirsty for more of Him.

When I find that my passion for Him seems more like a slow simmer than an all-consuming fire, I listen again to the words of S. M. Lockridge, the beloved pastor of forty years (1953–1993) at Calvary Baptist Church in San Diego, California. This is an excerpt, but you can hear the entire message in his own words on YouTube. You will be blessed.

That's My King

My Bible says my King is the King of the Jews.
He's the King of Israel.
He's the King of righteousness.
He's the King of the ages.
He's the King of heaven. He's the King of glory.
He's the King of Kings, and He's the Lord of Lords.
That's my King.
I wonder—do you know Him?

My King is a sovereign king.
No means of measure can define His limitless love.
He's enduringly strong. He's entirely sincere.
He's eternally steadfast. He's immortally graceful.
He's imperially powerful. He's impartially merciful.
Do you know Him?

He's the greatest phenomenon that has ever crossed the horizon of this world.
He's God's Son.
He's a sinner's Savior.
He's the centerpiece of civilization.
He's unparalleled. He's unprecedented.
He's the loftiest idea in literature.
He's the highest personality in philosophy.
He's the fundamental doctrine in true theology.
He's the only One qualified to be an all-sufficient Savior.
I wonder if you know Him today!

He supplies strength for the weak.
He's available for the tempted and the tried.
He sympathizes, and He saves.
He strengthens and sustains.
He guards, and He guides.
He heals the sick. He cleanses the lepers.
He forgives sinners. He discharges debtors.
He delivers the captive. He defends the feeble.
He blesses the young. He serves the unfortunate.

He regards the aged. He rewards the diligent. He beautifies the meager.
I wonder if you know Him.

He's the key to knowledge.
He's the wellspring of wisdom.
He's the doorway of deliverance.
He's the pathway of peace.
He's the roadway to righteousness.
He's the highway to holiness. He's the gateway of glory.
Do you know Him?

His life is matchless. His goodness is limitless.
His mercy is everlasting. His love never changes.
His Word is enough. His grace is sufficient.
His reign is righteous.
His yoke is easy, and His burden is light.
I wish I could describe Him to you.

He's indescribable.
He's incomprehensible.
He's invincible. He's irresistible.
You can't get Him off your mind.
You can't get Him off your hands.
You can't outlive Him. You can't live without Him.
The Pharisees couldn't stand Him,
But they found out they couldn't stop Him.
Pilot couldn't find any fault in Him.
Herod couldn't kill Him.
And the grave couldn't hold Him.
That's my King!
Yes, that's my King!

Just reading it again fills me with awe. Did it make you want to shout, "Hallelujah"?

Now let's look at what Scripture says about us. If you are a disciple of Christ, then you have acknowledged your sin; accepted Christ's payment for that sin, given out of His love for you; and turned away from sin with a heart of thanksgiving. If so, then these things are true of you:

- You are not your own, you were bought at a price (1 Cor. 6:19–20).
- You died with Christ (Col. 2:20).

- You are no longer condemned, for Christ set you free from the law of sin and death (Rom. 8:1-2).
- You have been made righteous (2 Cor. 5:21).
- You are a new creation (2 Cor. 5:21).
- You are firmly rooted in Christ, being built up in Him (Colossians 2:7).
- You have been given the mind of Christ (1 Cor. 2:16).
- You have been made complete in Christ (Col. 2:10 NLT).
- Your body is the temple of the Holy Spirit (1 Cor. 3:16).
- You have access to the Father through the Holy Spirit (Eph. 2:18).
- You are to purify yourself from anything that contaminates body and spirit (2 Cor. 7:1).
- You have been given everything you need for life and godliness through His divine power (2 Peter 1:3).
- You can participate in His divine nature and escape the corruption in the world (2 Pet. 1:4).
- You are an ambassador of Christ (2 Cor. 5:20).
- You have been given spiritual gifts (1 Cor. 12:1–11).
- You are to use your gifts to bring others to Christ and to build up the church (2 Cor. 5:18–20; 1 Cor. 14:12).

Wow! That's why we can live victoriously.

When you come to the Word, begin with a prayer that the Spirit will open your heart and mind to receive what He has for you today, for His truth is "spiritually discerned" (1 Cor. 2:14). If you do not have a particular Bible study method, or if you never have read through the whole Bible, I encourage you to start with the gospel of John. Do not rush to buy a "fill-in-the-blank" Bible study workbook. Instead, begin by reading the Word for yourself, with help from the Holy Spirit.

First John 2:20, 27 tells us, " . . . You have an anointing from the Holy One, and all of you know the truth . . . the anointing you received from him remains in you, and you do not need anyone to teach you . . . his anointing teaches you about all things. . . ."

You may find the following Bible study tool helpful.

WEAVING SCRIPTURE INTO THE **FABRIC** OF YOUR LIFE

FABRIC is an acronym to help you meditate on Scripture as you read. Allow God's Word to transform the very FABRIC of your life by asking these questions as you read a passage of Scripture. Not every question will apply to every scripture. Take time to allow the Holy Spirit to reveal truth to you. This is very important, so don't rush. Write your responses in your journal, and then pray that God will empower you to live in obedience. His revelation and your obedience will lead to transformation, progressively conforming you to the image of Christ.

F—What *fact* do I need to receive by faith?
A—What *attitude* do I need to adjust?
B—What *behavior* needs repentance?
R—What *response* would be God-honoring?
I—What *insight* needs more prayer and meditation?
C—What *concept* needs more clarification?

Try it with this passage of Scripture:

His divine power has given us everything we need for life and godliness through our knowledge of him who called us by his own glory and goodness. Through these he has given us his very great and precious promises, so that through them you may participate in the divine nature and escape the corruption in the world caused by evil desires.

—2 Peter 1:3–4

Let me share my own example:

Fact—God's divine power already has given me everything I need to live a life of godliness, and I actually can participate in His divine nature. What an awesome truth. It is beyond imagining!

Attitude—Because He has given me everything I need for life and godliness, I can live in victory and not with an attitude of discouragement, despair, or defeat.

Behavior—I do not have to participate in the corruption of the world. Therefore, I will choose not to watch mindless, morally jaded movies and television programs or read books and magazines that promote a godless worldview.

Response—I want to share this powerful truth this week with the young woman I mentor.

Insight—I no longer can use my personality as an excuse for my behavior and attitudes.

Concept—What are the "very great and precious promises" Peter talks about here? I need further inquiry.

I believe this passage of Scripture is one of the most profound truths in our quest for holiness. Spend time over the next several weeks meditating on it, until it penetrates your soul. It can be life-changing.

Warren Wiersbe wrote this powerful statement: "If divine truth doesn't touch our own hearts and affect our conduct, then our Bible study is only an intellectual exercise to inflate our own ego."[7] Ponder that one for a while!

STUDY RESOURCES

After you have developed a regular habit of reading the Word, you will find it helpful to add additional study resources. A Bible dictionary and/or encyclopedia, an exhaustive concordance, and commentaries are all of value, but they must *never* replace a personal reading of the Word under the guidance of the Holy Spirit. I love having my books at my fingertips so I can highlight and make notes in the margins, but many of these resources are now available on the Internet and often are free. Use your search engine for a wonderful time of exploring the ever-increasing biblical resources online.

JOURNALING

Even if you are not particularly thrilled with the thought of writing, I strongly suggest you use a journal to record your thoughts and discovered treasures of truth. Adele Ahlberg Calhoun writes, "Journaling is a way of paying attention to our lives . . . . On the pages of a journal, in the privacy of a moment, we can take tentative steps into truth and scour our feelings, hurts, ideas, and struggles before God."[8]

SCRIPTURE MEMORY

As you study the Word, I suggest you keep a stack of three-by-five cards near your Bible and begin writing out those verses that you feel led to memorize. Carry them in your purse or in your car and use any "down time" in the carpool lane or doctor's office to work on your memory verses. They will calm your spirit in times of crisis, provide power for your prayers, and give you boldness in your witness.

First Peter 3:15b tells us, "Always be prepared to give an answer to everyone who asks you to give the reason for the hope that you have."

CAUTION!

As you pursue truth, I caution you not to make the mistake many believers have made over the years, sometimes causing them to walk away from the faith. Please ask yourself whether a particular scripture presents a *principle*, a *promise*, or a *precept*.

- A *principle* is a standard that, when followed, is likely to lead to a specific outcome. Example: if you eat natural foods that are rich in vitamins and minerals and exercise regularly, you are likely to enjoy greater health than someone who does not.
- A *promise* is an assurance that what has been declared will become reality. Example: I promise to love, honor, and cherish my husband until death. If it is a promise, is it to a specific people, nation, or person for a specific time? Or is it a generalized promise to all believers? Example: "If we confess our sins, he is faithful and just and will forgive us our sins and cleanse us from all unrighteousness" (1 John 1:9) is a promise to all believers.
- A *precept*, as it is used in Scripture, is a rule or set of instructions that will guide moral behavior. Example: "You shall have no other Gods before me (Ex. 20:3 and Deut 5:7). Some verses have a precept *and* a promise. The passage from 1 John contains both. The precept is that we are to confess our sins; the promise is that He will forgive our sins.

Confusion reigns if we do not understand this difference. If we take a principle and claim it as a promise, we have disappointment waiting for us just around the corner. If this happens too often, we begin to doubt the very Word of God. Let me give a few examples.

As the mother of a "prodigal," I was told by well-meaning members of the Christian community that I just needed to claim the truth that when we train up a child in the way he should go, when he is old he will not turn from it (Prov. 22:6). Let me ask you, have you ever known parents who were godly role models, raised their children in the Word and in the fellowship of the church, and yet had a child who rebelled and died without receiving Christ? Was this verse a principle, a promise, or a precept?

Or how about the many people who claim Jeremiah 29:11 as their personal promise, "For I know the plans I have for you . . . plans to prosper you and not to harm you, plans to give you a hope and a future." I love that verse as well as anyone, but it was not a promise for all believers. It was written to the Israelites, who were exiled in Babylon. It was a promise for Israel as a "nation" and not for the individual Jew to claim. In verse 10, just before it, the Word says, "When seventy years are completed for Babylon, I will come to you and fulfill my gracious promise to bring you back to this place." Then it goes on to say, " . . . I know the plans I have for you." When we take a verse out of context and claim it as a promise, we can lead people astray.

If Jeremiah 29:11 were a promise to all believers, think about John the Baptist. Here he was, sitting in prison because he spoke truth to Herod when he told him it was not lawful for him to have his brother's wife. John was a man of impeccable character. Jesus even confirmed that, saying, "Among those born of women there has not risen anyone greater than John the Baptist" (Matt. 11:11). And yet, what was John's reality? It was as if God said, "I know the plans I have for you, John; plans for you to prepare the way for my Son, and to be beheaded when you are done" (my words, not Scripture). Please don't think I am being blasphemous or irreverent, but instead, listen to my heart. God chose not to intervene in John's plight.

John was an obedient servant; yet his life on earth was short, and he died on the orders of a cruel tyrant, at the request of a dancing girl, who was manipulated by her adulterous mother (Matthew 14:1–12). Life for an obedient disciple of Christ does not come with a promise of hope for a prosperous future, at least not in this life.

Let me share a personal experience with this issue, from when I used to cling to that "promise" from Jeremiah. In 2005, I was back in Africa, planning to train a women's leadership team in Community Health Evangelism. I had spent considerable time, money, and effort to prepare for this ministry. I thought I was within God's will; yet from the moment my feet touched African soil, everything that could go wrong did. Due to fuel shortages, power outages, equipment failures, and physical illnesses, we accomplished nothing.

Attempting to salvage something from this disastrous trip, I got out of bed on a Monday morning, feeling that perhaps I was beyond the worst of the illness, and walked for fifteen minutes to the school to present an introductory computer workshop to a few of the teachers. I did well until about 11 A.M., when the symptoms returned with a vengeance. In a panic, I abruptly excused myself as warm liquid began running down my legs.

Walking as fast as I could to the guesthouse, as there were no plumbing facilities at the school, I noticed that the aromatic fluid now was filling my shoes. Every step was a "squish." I prayed that I would not meet anyone on the road, which would require me to stop and give a proper greeting. As I rounded the bend, with the guesthouse in sight, a donkey cart and driver were crossing the path. The donkey put his nose in the air, sniffed a few times, shook his head, and looked around for the source of the pungent odor. Then he looked directly at me and snorted with distain. How humiliating! Could it get any worse?

It was just a few days before we were to leave, and I was back in bed, weaker than I ever had been. Then an e-mail came to the guesthouse after the power was restored, informing me that my dear friend and the director of our jail ministry was on life-support following a massive heart attack. She was not expected to live, and I was asked to speak at her funeral. It was my tipping point. My dear friend was only fifty-two, without any of the classic risk factors for heart disease. She had the greatest gift of evangelism I had ever personally encountered. Twelve women had come to Christ at the jail in just three months of her leadership, and they attended her Bible study each week.

"God, what are You doing?" I asked Him. "Why? What is Your purpose in all of this?" I not only felt physically and emotionally depleted, but also, spiritually, I was having a crisis of faith. "Where are You, God?"

I came back to North Carolina on a Friday, spoke at the funeral on Saturday, and later that day, crawled into an emotional and spiritual cave, wanting no contact or comfort. This was something just between God and me. I sought answers but found only silence. I emerged a few days later to go through the motions of my life, but I was not at all engaged.

I remained in that state of darkness for nearly a month. I began to feel jealous that my friend had gone on to be with the Lord and had left me here in such a state of confusion. "Where are You, Lord?" I asked. Then He spoke to my soul from the book of Job:

> Where were you when I laid the earth's foundation?
> Tell me, if you understand.
> Who marked off its dimensions?
> Surely you know!
> Who stretched a measuring line across it?
> On what were its footings set,
> Or who laid the cornerstone—
> While the morning stars sang together
> And all the angels shouted for joy? (Job 38:4–7)

> Have you ever given orders to the morning,
> Or shown the dawn its place? (Job 38:12)

> Have you ever journeyed to the springs of the sea
> Or walked in the recesses of the deep? (Job 38:16)

> Have you comprehended the vast expanses of the earth?
> Tell me if you know all this. (Job 38:18)

> Would you discredit my justice?
> Would you condemn me to justify yourself? (Job 40:8)

I felt ashamed. I had operated out of the assumption that God had a plan to prosper me and my ministry, and that He owed me an explanation if things did not turn out as I had expected they would. How foolish! How arrogant! How misled! You only need to look at the life of the apostle Paul to know that there are times when passionate, obedient disciples of Christ will suffer, and suffer intensely, but remain faithful still.

Lord, did Satan ask to sift me as wheat? Was I found lacking? Did I disappoint you? Oh, Father, forgive my frail and faltering faith. You are my God, and I will forever praise You with the psalmist: "I will praise you, O Lord, with all my heart; I will tell of all your wonders. I will be glad and rejoice in you; I will sing praise to your name, O Most High" (Ps. 9:1–2).

Action step: Describe your relationship with the Word of God up to this point in your story.

Reflection question: How would you like to describe that relationship five years from now?

Prayer: Spend time in prayer, reflecting and receiving what the Holy Spirit wants to reveal to you. *Respond in your journal.*

Chapter 19

Faith on its Knees in Prayer

SEVERAL YEARS AGO, I had the privilege of witnessing a passionate prayer warrior in action. We were on a return trip to Africa, and I was to attend a women's gathering on Saturday afternoon at two o'clock. Being a typical American, for whom time matters, I showed up at 1:45. The only other person there was the pastor's wife. We chatted awhile as we waited for the others to arrive.

At 2:30, no one else had come. I just assumed that it was the cultural pattern to disregard time and fully expected the women would trail in soon. The pastor's wife, however, sensed something different. She spoke of recent spiritual battles and decided she would have to "pray them in." She fell to her knees and began, softly at first, then with increasing intensity, to plead with the Holy Spirit to draw the women to the church. Because she prayed in her tribal tongue, I could not fully follow her prayer, but there was no mistaking her passion and her purpose. She did not rise from the floor until the women began to arrive—not just a few, but enough to fill the room.

When we had a chance to talk afterward, she said that many had forgotten, some had made other commitments, and a few had made the decision not to attend. But the power of the Holy Spirit began to draw them to the church. I was amazed, not at the response to her prayer, but at the faith that drove her to her knees. I want to be that kind of prayer warrior!

Without question, E. M. Bounds has been one of my greatest prayer mentors. He died in 1913, relatively unknown to most Christians, but his written legacy has impassioned generations of believers to seek intimacy with God in prayer. Bounds was a man deeply committed to prayer and made a habit of getting up at four o'clock in the morning to lift his burdens to God. His simplest definition of prayer is that it is both "communion and communication with God."[1]

Let's look at those two facets of prayer. The first is *communion* with God. As North American Christians, when we think of communion, we most likely think of the bread and wine that represent Christ's body and blood. But the Greek word for "communion" in the New Testament (KJV) is *koinonia*, which basically means fellowship. I like to think of it as being in His presence. But who can stand in God's presence? Psalm 5:5 tells us that the arrogant cannot stand in His presence. So, obviously, one of the criteria for being in fellowship with God is humility. We must come before Him knowing that we are unworthy, in our own right, to approach His holiness. That leads us to a heart of gratitude for His grace, and that reaffirms our love for God. It is love that creates the hunger and thirst to be in fellowship with Him. So let's review—humility, gratitude, and love, three essential attitudes in preparation for prayer.

Psalm 24:3 asks, "Who may ascend the hill of the Lord? Who may stand in his holy place?" We find the answer in verse four: "He who has clean hands and a pure heart. . . " This should lead us to a time of confession and repentance. Once we have acknowledged who He is and admitted who we are, that should lead us naturally to a time of praise.

Again, I think of Bounds's words: "To have God thus near is to enter the Holy of Holies—to breathe the fragrance of the heavenly air, to walk in Eden's delightful gardens. Nothing but prayer can bring God and man into this happy communion."[2]

Now we are ready for the second facet, *communication*. When it comes to communication with God, there is no better place to begin than in His Word. As we open His Word, we gain access to His truth, wisdom, correction, encouragement, instruction, and promises. We begin to understand His nature and His holiness. As a general practice, Scripture, prayer, and worship are so intertwined that it is difficult to separate them. Just as we don't ask the heart to stop beating so we can take a breath or ask the lungs to stop inhaling and exhaling so we can think, Scripture, prayer, and worship are a synergistic reality in the life of an authentic disciple of Christ.

Yet there will be times, particularly in a crisis, when you hardly can pray at all. When our son, Geoff, was fourteen years old, he went to the beach with our church youth group, and we went to South Carolina to visit family. Late into the night, we were awakened by the phone call that all parents dread. Geoff had been hit by a car as he was crossing the street with a group of friends. He was thrown into the air and landed across the median into oncoming traffic. At the time of the call, he was on his way to surgery, and we did not yet know the full extent of his injuries. I couldn't breathe! As I rushed to get dressed, all I could pray was, "Please, God. Please, God. Please, God." No other words would come.

We called our small group leader, who called the rest of the group, asking them to pray. As we headed to the hospital, about two hours away, a peace washed over us, the peace that passes all understanding. We knew our care group was interceding for us when we barely could pray for ourselves.

Geoff made an amazing recovery! Within weeks of his accident, he left with the youth group on a short-term mission trip. We serve an awesome God! But had God taken him that day, He still would be an awesome God. Our circumstances do not alter the truth of Who He is—ever!

> Thus in every circumstance of life, prayer is the most natural outpouring of the soul, the unhindered turning to God for communion and direction. Whether in sorrow or in joy, in defeat or in victory, in weakness or in health, in calamity or in success, the heart leaps to meet with God, just as a child runs to his mother's arms, ever sure that her sympathy will meet every need.[3]

SEASONS OF PRAYER

E. M. Bounds talks about "seasons of prayer," when we set aside time to shut out everything else that can distract us and focus solely on God. Without these times of deep, intentional intimacy, our spiritual lives can become stale and our prayers shallow. Time away allows us the freedom to linger before Him, waiting in anticipation for Him to reveal truth, provide clarity for important decisions, or draw us into deeper union with Himself. This slice of solitude can happen in a variety of ways, but we must be intentional. Even Jesus withdrew to a private place for time alone with His Father. What makes us think we do not need it?

In his book *Secrets of the Secret Place*, Bob Sorge says, "Intimacy precedes insight. Passion precedes purpose. First comes the secret place, then comes divine guidance . . . God's primary desire for your life is not that you discover His will and walk in it; His primary desire is that you draw near to Him and come to know Him . . . then He desires that from that knowing relationship there comes a tender walking together in His purposes."[4] Sorge goes on to say, "The closer we draw to the Lord in intimacy, the more real the warfare will be we encounter."[5]

Let's return to Bounds for his comments:

> Everything depends on prayer, and yet we neglect it—not only to our own spiritual hurt, but also to the delay and injury of our Lord's cause upon the earth. The forces of good and evil are contending for the world. If we would pray, we could add to the conquering power of the army of righteousness; and yet our lips are sealed, our hands hang listlessly by our sides, and by holding back from the prayer chamber we jeopardize the very cause in which we profess to be deeply interested.[6]

There is no way around it—prayer is the very power behind the faith we claim to profess. But do we know how to pray with power? I have thought for a long time now that prayer formulas seem inauthentic. If God is really our Father, we should not need a formula for communicating with Him. But I must admit that when I first began to seek a deeper understanding of prayer, I used the ACTS acronym that so often is taught to new believers: Adoration, Confession,

Thanksgiving, and Supplication. I didn't even know what supplication was. It simply means *requests*, but that wouldn't have made a very memorable acronym. Though I think a memorable formula, like ACTS, may be helpful to a new believer, as we mature in the faith, it is better to allow the Word and the Holy Spirit to guide our intimate time in prayer.

But prayer is more than just power to accomplish God's purposes.

> Prayer is the contact of a living soul with God. In prayer, God stoops to kiss man, to bless man, and to assist man in everything. . . . Prayer fills man's emptiness with God's fullness. It fills man's poverty with God's riches. It replaces man's weakness with God's strength. It banishes man's littleness with God's greatness. Prayer is God's plan to supply man's great and continuous need with God's great and continuous abundance.[7]

May you discover what Christ already knew—that "prayer was the secret of His power; the law of His life; the inspiration of His work; and the source of His wealth, His joy, His communion, and His strength."[8]

Action step: Describe your prayer life up to this point in your story.

Reflection question: How would you like to describe your prayer life five years from now?

Prayer: Spend time in prayer, reflecting and receiving what the Holy Spirit wants to reveal to you. *Respond in your journal.*

Chapter 2

A Lifestyle of Worship

WHAT COMES TO your mind when I say the word "worship"? If you are like most believers, the first thing that comes to mind is the Sunday morning worship service and, more specifically, the music. But is that the essence of worship? Is worship defined by a certain place, a particular practice, or worse yet, a performance? Warren Wiersbe writes, "If our concept of God is so low that we think He's pleased with cheap, halfhearted worship, then we don't know the God of the Bible."[1]

I believe it is very difficult to engage in community worship on Sunday morning until we have learned how to worship personally in our solitary place, our private sanctuary, the temple of the Holy Spirit. Here we come, stripped of all pretense and protection. It is here, in our solitary place, where we can learn to worship "in spirit and in truth" (John 4:24). Dallas Willard says, "In solitude, we confront our own soul with its obscure forces and conflicts that escape our attention when we are interacting with others . . . And yet what we find of him in that solitude enables us to return to society as free persons."[2] But how do we experience that?

First, as mentioned previously, we must come in humility, for the arrogant cannot stand in God's presence (Ps. 5:5). Then we must truly seek Him: "Oh, God, you are my God, earnestly I seek you; my soul thirsts for you, my body longs for you, in a dry and weary land where there is no water" (Ps. 63:1).

As we seek Him and come into His presence, we praise Him (Ps. 22:26) for Who He is:

- For His greatness (Deut. 32:3)
- For the splendor of His holiness (2 Chron. 20:21)
- For His love that endures forever (2 Chron. 20:21)

- For His compassion and mercy (James 5:11)
- For His faithfulness through all generations (Ps. 119:90)
- For His light that penetrates a dark world (John 8:12)

And, of course, the list can go on and on. As you study the Word, you can keep adding to these attributes of God on your three-by-five cards and use them in worship.

As we become aware of His holiness, we are driven to confession so that our hearts are pure before Him, which then leads us to thanksgiving for what He has done for us, in us, and through us. At this point, it is almost impossible not to be overwhelmed by emotion in this private sanctuary, where "Spirit touches spirit."[3]

When we have experienced that kind of private worship, what a joy it is to engage in corporate worship with our brothers and sisters in Christ, uniting our spirits to lift up our Lord, knowing that all across the nations, fellow believers are rejoicing with us as the worldwide body of Christ. The power of that reality is beyond words!

Action step: Describe your experience with worship up to this point in your story.

Reflection question: How would you like to describe your experience with worship five years from now?

Prayer: Spend time in prayer, reflecting and receiving what the Holy Spirit wants to reveal to you. *Respond in your journal.*

Chapter 21

Following Jesus in Service

IT WAS A hot, humid day. I was driving away from the nursing home after visiting my mother, and I was complaining to the Lord about His lack of direction for the rest of my life. As I neared the church, I saw a long-time member of the congregation mowing the back lot. Sweat rolled down his face as he pushed with perseverance, back and forth.

I stopped, rolled down my window, and said in jest, "Jerry, is that in your job description?" He turned off the mower and ambled to my window. What he said next changed the way I think about service in the kingdom of God.

"Well, it's like this," he said. "I'm not one of those folk who know for sure what I'm supposed to be doing. I have never felt a particular call from God, so I figure I just better look around and see what needs doing and do it."

Jerry has served on just about every board in the church. Some Sundays you'll find him rolling wheelchair patients from the nursing home down to the worship service. Several months ago, he helped organize a fundraiser for our mission project in Zambia. You see, Jerry is one of those believers filled to overflowing. Recently, he was honored for his forty-five years of service teaching Sunday school. The pastor asked all those who had been touched by Jerry's ministry to stand. All over the sanctuary, people stood, until it seemed that half the congregation was on its feet. Then they broke into spontaneous applause. I still get choked up just writing about it. Jerry is truly one of the most humble men I know.

Jesus said, "Whoever wants to become great among you must be your servant, and whoever wants to be first must be slave of all. For even the Son of Man did not come to be served, but to serve, and to give his life as a ransom for many" (Mark 10:43–45).

Whether he is mowing the back lot at the church, teaching Sunday school, staining a fence at the shelter for homeless women, or sharing Christ with someone who has resisted the truth for years, Jerry pours himself out as a drink offering—not because he is earning points on his heavenly scorecard, but because he is so filled with Christ that he is compelled to serve. His lifestyle simply reflects the life of Christ that abides in him.

Disciples of Christ are most effective when they fulfill three areas of responsibility in the kingdom of God.

1. Ambassadors of Christ—who accept His call to be engaged in the ministry of reconciliation.
2. Advocates for the church—who promote unity in the body of Christ, make disciples, give of their financial resources, and serve the church with their unique gifts and abilities.
3. Activists in the community—who feed the hungry, house the homeless, visit the imprisoned, care for the orphans and widows, and fight for justice for the oppressed, both locally and globally.

Let's look at each of these roles and responsibilities in greater depth.

AMBASSADOR OF CHRIST

As an ambassador of Christ, each of us is called to the ministry of reconciliation (2 Cor. 5:18). But what exactly does that mean? The Greek word used for "reconciliation" is *katallage*, which essentially means a restored relationship to God. We are to be engaged in ministry that helps sinners find their way back into a right relationship with God. In the language of the church, we might call this evangelism.

When I hear the word "evangelism," my mind immediately goes to the person who walks up to a complete stranger and says, "If you were to die tonight, do you know where you will spend eternity?" The thought of such a "reconciliation approach" makes my heart race and my breathing labored. I never have done that, and I probably never will. But I have discovered that the more intimate I am with the Lord, the more natural spiritual conversations have become.

I might have a spiritual encounter in the grocery store, during a tutoring session, or as the result of a simple question like, "How are you, *really*?" I might follow it up with an invitation to church, the gift of a paperback New Testament, or a long conversation over coffee. The Holy Spirit's promptings determine whom I speak to and how I follow up. As His ambassador, I am His "free agent," always available and always open to a change of plans according to His purposes. Let me give you a personal example.

We were nearly finished with building the log cabin, and I began wondering how I would decorate it for Christmas, as it would become our holiday gathering place. At a Christmas craft fair, I met a woman who was selling beautiful, handmade Santas. I really liked the way she decorated her booth, so I asked if I could hire her to give me some decorating ideas for the cabin. When she arrived in the country, she noticed the plaques of Scripture tucked here and there and mentioned that she did not grow up in a church and knew very little about the Bible. Sensing a divine encounter, I put on a pot of coffee. We sat on the sofa while I shared my testimony and invited her to the Christmas production at our church. It was the start of a wonderful walk of faith. She and her husband became active members of a church in their community, engaged in Bible study, and served joyfully wherever they were needed. It was not what I had planned for the day, but it fit the Lord's agenda perfectly, and I had a new friend and sister in Christ.

Author Kenneth Boa, in *Conformed to His Image*, states, "We are charged to be ambassadors of the King . . . and when we take this commission seriously, we find that our souls are enlarged by embracing a clear sense of destiny and purpose. When we are on the King's business as agents of reconciliation, we develop a kingdom mentality and order our lives in accordance with our Lord's purposes."[1]

Scripture tells us: ". . . always be prepared to give an answer to everyone who asks you to give the reason for the hope that you have. But do this with gentleness and respect" (1 Pet. 3:15). The expectation is that we will prepare. We must begin by being able to share our personal story of reconciliation. Can you share your testimony in five minutes?

ADVOCATE FOR THE CHURCH

As advocates for the church, we contribute to the health and well-being of our local congregation by promoting unity, making disciples, giving of our financial resources, finding our unique fit for ministry, and using our gifts and talents to advance the kingdom.

Unity

Have you ever belonged to a church that suffered from disunity? Like a dysfunctional family, it is painful, shameful, and unbiblical. You surely don't want to invite anyone in to sense the tension, observe the hostility, or overhear the criticism and condemnation. Sadly, there are far too many examples of how *not* to be the church.

As advocates for the church, we need to know what Scripture says about the body of Christ and how essential unity is to our Lord. Consider these Bible verses:

> I have given them the glory that you gave me, that they may be one as we are one: I in them and you in me. May they be brought to complete unity to let the world know that you sent me and have loved them even as you have loved me.
>
> —John 17:22–23

Now you are the body of Christ, and each one of you is a part of it. There should be no division in the body. . . . If one part suffers, every part suffers with it; if one part is honored, every part rejoices with it.

—1 Corinthians 12:27, 25–26

May the God who gives endurance and encouragement give you a spirit of unity among yourselves as you follow Christ Jesus, so that with one heart and mouth you may glorify the God and Father of our Lord Jesus Christ.

—Romans 15:5

Make every effort to keep the unity of the Spirit through the bond of peace. There is one body and one Spirit—just as you were called to one hope when you were called—one lord, one faith, one baptism; one God and Father of all, who is over all and through all and in all.

—Ephesians 4:3–6

Is there any question about how important unity is in the church? Is unity something we work toward, or is it the outcome of a gathering of saints who have surrendered themselves fully to the cross of Christ and fully received the gift of the Holy Spirit, whose love binds us all together in perfect unity? (See Col. 3:14.)

We must be careful not to mistake unity for uniformity. We do not all have to look alike, think alike, worship alike, or lead alike. We don't all have to be from the same economic, educational, or ethnic background. Diversity is both healthy and desirable. Remember that one day we will all be together—believers from every tongue and tribe and nation. Let's begin to enjoy each other now, so we don't miss out on the blessings.

Perhaps you are truly blessed and belong to a healthy, harmonious church. Then I ask you, how well does your local church engage with other churches in your community? Is there a sense of cooperation or competition? Is there an interdenominational effort to build partnerships in ministry, or are the churches working independently, unaware and unconcerned for the unity of the whole body of Christ?

Just think of the power of the entire body of Christ coming together to focus on issues in the community—sharing resources, serving together, praying together, and praising together. Shouldn't we stand together "against the rulers, against the authorities, against the powers of this dark world and against the spiritual forces of evil in the heavenly realms"? (See Eph. 6:12.)

A. W. Tozer says, "Unity is necessary among the children of God if we are going to know the flow of power."[2] He continues, "Revivals, whether big or small, have been mainly this: the achieving of a oneness of mind among a number of Christians."[3] Charles Colson, author and prison evangelist, says, "It would be refreshing if, instead of squabbling with one another, churches were to join hands in meeting community or social needs."[4] What power there is in unity! I believe that denominationalism has been used effectively by the enemy as a weapon to divide us, depleting our power and distracting us from our purpose. What a tragedy! It leads one to ask: What can we do about it?

Discipleship

As believers, each of us is called to "make disciples." Kenneth Boa writes, "The believer's highest call in ministry is to reproduce the life of Christ in others."[5] He goes on to say, "One of life's deepest satisfactions is witnessing the gradual miracle of transformation in converts who are serious about becoming disciples. By contrast, the mediocrity of non-discipleship cuts off the fruit of the Spirit and leads to a lack of love, joy, and peace."[6]

But just exactly what is discipleship, and what is our part in it? Discipleship is *not* a one-time event; it is a process. It is *not* a one-size-fits-all process; it is a personal timeline of transformation. And it is *not* something *we* do. It is something the *Holy Spirit* does, but we are allowed the privilege of being His vessels of truth, encouragement, accountability, and prayer. We do this in several ways:

- We are to *model* the life of Christ. Young believers want to know if the truth we profess is also the truth we live. They need to see us in everyday situations in our homes and during family activities. We must welcome them into our lives.
- We can *mentor* young believers, meeting one-on-one or in small groups for Bible study and prayer. You also can meet over coffee or a cola to discuss what is going on in her life, providing biblical perspective.
- We can *mobilize* resources that can address a young believer's specific needs. Here are some examples:

  - Provide childcare and a scholarship to send a single mother to a Christian parenting seminar.
  - Organize a weekend retreat for new Christians, with the purpose of building relationships with mature believers.
  - Plan a packing party for a young believer who is moving to a new apartment, surrounding her with love in action.

Discipleship requires time, energy, and focused prayer, but ultimately, the transformation is the work of the Holy Spirit. We must be careful not to try controlling the process or the outcome.

A few words of caution here: it is important to set boundaries on your time. Do not encourage the idea that the woman you are mentoring has twenty-four-hour access to you and your listening ear. She should not become dependent on you; she must develop dependence on the

Holy Spirit. This is very difficult for someone who likes to be needed. If that is your motive, you are not ready for one-on-one discipleship.

In 1999, we launched a women's mentoring ministry. We brought in a special speaker, developed a training program, and organized an afternoon tea, where women could meet potential mentors. Then a team of us prayed over the applications and matched the women, who then committed to meeting regularly for discipleship.

Though our intentions were good, we created an artificial process. Now don't misunderstand me. I am a big believer in "equipping the saints," but we were rather presumptuous in trying to match the women. When you have a heart for discipleship and are receptive to the Holy Spirit, He will reveal to you someone who needs your unique ability to share truth in such a way that it will be received and not resented.

There are varying seasons of our lives, each one with its own supply of expendable time and energy. Not everyone will be able to make the investment in one-on-one discipleship at this time, but each of us is called to be part of the process. Eventually, it should become a way of life for each of us.

Stewardship

When I was a young mother in my early twenties, we lived next door to a unique couple. I knew nothing about their faith, but they taught me a spiritual lesson about commitment and sacrifice that continues to convict me today. This couple had two children, and when those kids were still toddlers, the couple began a lifestyle of sacrifice and saving in order to build a college fund for them. When most of the other families were moving out of that neighborhood of starter homes, they stayed on to continue investing in the college fund because it was that important to them.

It wasn't that important to their kids, however. So when it came time to apply for college and neither child wanted to go, the parents made an amazing decision! They donated every dime of it to a scholarship fund for children of working class families. Their kids ranted and raged. They thought they might be able to use the money for a car or a down payment on a house, but the parents stood firm. This was a college fund. It would be used to send two high school kids to college, whether or not their own kids chose to take advantage of it. Now that is conviction! What a wonderful model of sacrifice and commitment to a higher good.

As Christians, we have the potential to sacrifice for the highest good—the eternal work of the kingdom. But sadly, most of us are saving for a new car, the next vacation, or a bigger house. What motivated the couple next door to sacrifice and save and then give it all away? Conviction.

What will it take to convict Christians to use their resources for kingdom purposes? More guilt-driven videos of African children dying of starvation? More sermons about stewardship from the pulpit? I don't believe so. When we love the Lord with all our hearts, minds, souls, and strength, and love our neighbors as ourselves, generosity will be the natural outcome of a heart fully devoted to following the Master.

What about the tithe? Isn't that all that's required? Gleaning a clear picture of the nature and function of the tithe in biblical times is difficult because of inconsistent accounts of the practice. Some Bible scholars believe that the Old Testament tradition of giving ten percent of yearly income was actually a tax collected at the temple, primarily to support the priests and Levites.[7] Though it was considered mandatory, it was not always observed or enforced.

I've heard many Christians say that as the New Testament church, we are no longer required to live by Old Testament mandates. And doesn't Scripture say, "Each man should give what he has decided in his heart to give, not reluctantly or under compulsion . . ." (2 Cor. 9:7)? Well, one thing is for sure. The average North American Christian does not feel any compulsion to tithe. A survey conducted in 2007 by George Barna's research group revealed that of all "born-again" adults, only nine percent tithe.[8]

Let me re-phrase that: ninety-one percent of all born-again adults *do not* tithe. I believe that if the church today were truly living as the early New Testament church, we would not only tithe, but also we would understand that *everything* we have been given belongs to the Lord and is to be used for His purposes. I wonder, would we even have a need for a government welfare system? That may sound rather radical, but listen again to the words of Scripture.

> All the believers were one in heart and mind. No one claimed that any of his possessions was his own, but they shared everything they had. With great power the apostles continued to testify to the resurrection of the Lord Jesus, and much grace was upon them all. There were no needy persons among them. For from time to time those who owned lands or houses sold them, brought the money from the sales and put it at the apostles' feet, and it was distributed to anyone as he had need.
>
> —Acts 4:32–35

How would you like to belong to that kind of church? What a comforting thought if you were in need. But what if you were among the wealthier church members? If you had an "ownership mentality" instead of a "stewardship mentality," it could be quite stressful. You might become resentful as you felt pressure from others to give, like Ananias and his wife, Sapphira, did. They were not required to give, but they wanted to be seen as generous, so they made a great display of giving. But they hoarded some for themselves and lied about it (Acts 5:1–11). It was all about the image.

In contrast, when you are filled with the love of Christ, conformed to His character, and committed to living authentically, the natural outflow will be generosity. I love the financial vision that Craig Groeschel describes in his book *Chazown*:

You're completely debt free. . . . No car payments. No credit card payments. Not even a house payment. You are not bound to a particular job (because income doesn't direct you). You have more than enough for your needs; you even enjoy certain luxuries as blessings from God. You pay cash for everything. You've been faithful with little, so God has entrusted you with much. You are therefore free to give as God leads you, even funding entire ministries. When you see someone in need, you immediately help. Your answer to God is simply "yes." For the rest of your life.[9]

Two-thirds of Jesus' parables spoke directly about money or possessions, so we have to assume that He was warning us of the great danger that material possessions and financial distractions can become competitors for our hearts.[10]

I recently read the following quote and found it so piercing that I pass it on to you: "The real value of money is its ability to reveal what is in our hearts."[11]

Ministry

In 2003, our senior pastor called me into his office and asked if I would be willing to consider a part-time staff position to "mobilize the laity." I wondered what he had in mind and asked for greater clarity. His response was, "I want you to create 'on ramps' to get people serving in the church."

I was leaving for Africa later that week, so I told him I would pray about it and get back with him when I returned. After much disquiet, as I was a bit overwhelmed by the challenge, I agreed to accept the position. Not having a clue how to begin, I called other large churches for advice. Then we bought volunteer tracking software, created purpose statements for the various ministry opportunities, and developed a workshop to help people find their perfect "fit" for ministry.

We thought we had done it "right," yet few people were serving. Sure, they came out for the workshops to discover their divine design, but few followed through with the placement process. Many said that they had not felt a "call" from the Lord, so they just would wait. This is so common in the church today.

What are we waiting for? An audible voice? A vision in the clouds? A burning bush experience? Os Guinness, in his book *The Call*, distinguishes between our *primary calling* and our *secondary calling:*

Our primary calling as followers of Christ is by him, to him, and for him. First and foremost we are called to Someone (God), not to something (such as motherhood, politics, or teaching) or to somewhere (such as the inner city or Outer Mongolia). [12]

Our secondary calling, considering who God is as sovereign, is that everyone, everywhere, and in everything should think, speak, live, and act entirely for him. We can therefore properly say as a matter of secondary calling that we are called to homemaking or to the practice of law or to art history. . . . They are our personal answer to God's address, our response to God's summons. Secondary callings matter, but only because the primary calling matters most.[13]

Guinness makes a further distinction between our *ordinary calling* and a *special calling*:

A special calling refers to those tasks and missions laid on an individual through a direct, specific, supernatural communication from God. Ordinary calling, on the other hand, is the believer's sense of life-purpose and life-task in response to God's primary call, "follow me," even when there is no direct, specific, supernatural communication from God about a secondary calling.[14]

Guinness also points out another aspect of calling: "God normally calls us along the line of our giftedness, but the purpose of giftedness is stewardship and service, not selfishness."[15]

When we shift our thinking to "ours" instead of "mine" or "hers," we can overcome any sense of pride or envy when evaluating giftedness. Let me give an example. I love to sing. It is one of my favorite forms of worship. I have been singing in church choirs for over thirty years. But, alas, I have not been given a beautiful solo voice. Early in my walk with the Lord, when I heard an incredible voice that had the power to bring tears to my eyes and a lump to my throat, I felt a sense of envy. Since I have come to understand God's gifts, I now can close my eyes during such worship and rejoice in the gift that belongs to "us" and thank Him for the blessing.

I have come to understand that people don't serve, at least not very effectively or for very long, just because there is a need. Believers seek and find effective ministry opportunities when they understand that their primary calling is to Christ and are so full of Him that the overflow compels them to minister.

We will explore your unique fit for ministry in the church and the community, both locally and globally, in Part Four. But first, let's take a look at our role as activists in the community.

ACTIVIST IN THE COMMUNITY

Recently my husband and I attended a small Sunday school class of twenty to twenty-four people, all very committed to the church—kind and loving people, any of whom would lend a hand in a crisis. We were discussing community outreach, and when the facilitator asked how many in the class were involved in volunteer service in the community on a regular basis, only one other hand went up in response. I was stunned.

Craig Groeschel, pastor of Life Church in Oklahoma, had a similar experience when he surveyed about fifty Christians and asked the question, "If money were no object, what would you do for the rest of your life?"

Fully expecting people to say they would serve others, perhaps volunteer in a crisis pregnancy center, mentor inner-city kids, or adopt a child from a developing country, he was dismayed at their answers. Instead of Spirit-led responses, those surveyed had more self-focused dreams. They would quit work and travel, buy a new car or a nice house, or hire household help.[16]

Christ clearly calls us to a different path, a radical path of selfless service. Let's look at the illustration of the sheep and the goats in Matthew 25:31–46. I invite you to grab your Bible and take the time right now to read it.

When Christ comes in all His glory, He will sit on His throne, and the nations will gather before Him. And, like a shepherd who knows his sheep, He easily will separate them from the goats and invite them to take their inheritance, the kingdom prepared for them since the creation of the world. By what criteria will He separate them? I had assumed it would be those whose sins were forgiven and covered by the blood of the Lamb. End of story. But there is more to the story. The criteria He used in the Matthew passage were the services to "the least of these": the hungry, the thirsty, the naked, the sick, the imprisoned, and the stranger. He sent the "goats," who had failed to respond to the needs before them, into eternal punishment and the righteous "sheep" to eternal life.

I don't know about you, but this disturbed me. I thought it was all about *grace* and not about *works*. So how do we reconcile this dilemma? Let's turn to the book of James.

Religion that God our Father accepts as pure and faultless is this: to look after orphans and widows in their distress and to keep oneself from being polluted by the world.

—James 1:27

But someone will say, "You have faith; I have deeds." Show me your faith without deeds, and I will show you my faith by what I do.

—James 2:18

As the body without the spirit is dead, so faith without deeds is dead.

—James 2:26

It is not that we earn our salvation through works, but rather, we *demonstrate* our authentic faith through the choices we make. If we are His sheep, then we listen to His voice and follow Him (John 10:27). In John 15:8 we read, "This is to my Father's glory, that you bear much fruit, showing yourselves to be my disciples."

Those of us who grew up in evangelical churches were taught that the "fruit" refers to souls that are saved. So does that mean that all our works are worthless unless they result in a saved soul? Matthew 25:31–46 says nothing about salvation being the outcome of our service. It is all about our works of compassion to those in need. Christ's love compels us (2 Cor. 5:14), so we serve because we are filled with the "fruit of the Spirit." When we minister through the Spirit, it is a powerful ministry of "love, joy, peace, patience, kindness, goodness, faithfulness, gentleness, and self-control" (Gal. 5:22–23). Of course, as an ambassador of Christ, you should always "be prepared to give an answer to everyone who asks you to give a reason for the hope that you have" (1 Pet. 3:15), but we are to leave the results to the Holy Spirit. If you do not grasp this truth, your ministry as an activist in the community will carry with it a burden of always having to measure the outcomes. When that happens, your ministry becomes a program rather than a lifestyle of love and Christ-like ministry. I promise you that when you serve out of Christ's love, it is so compelling that others will be drawn to know this Christ, Whom you serve.

In their book *2020 Vision*, Bill and Amy Stearnes write:

> It is clear from Scripture that the church isn't called to choose *either* evangelism *or* social action, as some have polarized these efforts. Others have paralleled the efforts, with the suggestion that both areas of blessing have the same motivation of love, so they can be emphasized as separate but equal ministries. But we can move beyond both . . . to a prioritizing of evangelism and social action.[17]

Warren Wiersbe, in his book *On Being a Servant of God*, says, "Ministry takes place when divine resources meet human needs through loving channels to the glory of God."[18] We are the channels through which divine resources are distributed. If we become warehouses instead of distribution centers, the work of the body of Christ suffers from a form of famine, while the hungry eyes of the lost around us search for fulfillment in all the wrong places.

Where do we begin our ministry as activists in the community? Start in your own community. Gather a small team together to begin making contacts in the community. Assess what other churches, agencies, or non-profits are doing to meet human needs. Are there ministries that need volunteers and resources that your church can provide? Or are there obvious gaps in services that may need a new, focused ministry team? Gather members of your church and community together for a time of praying, brainstorming, and dreaming. Let me share what happened when a faithful few in our community chose this path.

Our church is only blocks away from what used to be one of the highest crime districts in our city. Drugs, prostitution, and violence were an everyday reality for the west end, and three neighborhood churches had had enough. Working together, and with significant support from the police department, they launched West End Ministries, an interdenominational ministry to the hurting people of the west end.

The ministry provides adult life skills classes, a children's after school program, a food pantry and thrift shop, and a weekly community meal. Recently, with funds from additional area churches, they built a shelter for homeless women. West End Ministries has become a model of community action and Christian compassion. It has greater dreams yet. They are hoping more churches will provide volunteers who are willing to commit to one-on-one tutoring and discipleship, a personal investment in the life of someone not likely to be found in your typical church fellowship.

Working in your community is a great way to learn about servanthood. But I caution you—the role of servant takes a while to master. Want to know how well you have learned this lesson? Ask yourself how you would respond if you were treated like a servant.

When you have learned your lessons well locally, Christ may open up international opportunities of service for you. Let me tell you the story of a woman I deeply admire and respect.

Jo Anne Lyon is an ordained pastor, married to a pastor, and a mother of four grown children. She was working as the clinical director of a four-county mental health system, when she knew it was time to pursue a dream. Always a woman of compassion, she became involved in the organization Evangelicals for Social Action and began to get a vision of what she could do "to empower people economically and educationally at a grassroots level."[19]

She had a vision for a ministry, with no funds to support it. But believing that nothing is impossible with God, she quit her job and, in 1996, established the first office of World Hope International in a bedroom vacated by one of her grown children. As each of the kids moved away, she claimed yet another room for the budding ministry. Since that early one-room beginning, World Hope International has served in more than thirty countries and has touched the lives of nearly one million people.[20] Jo Anne has become a world-changer, raising awareness, raising funds, raising up leaders, raising the quality of life for "the least of these," and always raising up the name of Christ. She is a vital activist in the community worldwide.

Have you begun to get a vision of what life as an activist in the community will look like for you? Scripture gives you lots of options to choose from as you live out your "ordinary calling." We are to feed the hungry, house the homeless, visit the sick and imprisoned, care for orphans and widows, and work for the cause of justice wherever injustice reigns. Essentially, wherever a need exists, there is a need for Christ and His compassionate love, which provides the power and motive for ministry.

God has a "good work" for you to do. You are a unique combination of personality, values, passions, abilities, and spiritual gifts—your divine design. It is time to clarify your calling and take your place in the body of Christ as a "workman who does not need to be ashamed" (2 Tim. 2:15).

Action step: Describe your role as a servant of Christ up to this point in your story.

Reflection question: How would you like to describe it five years from now?

Prayer: Spend time in prayer, reflecting and receiving what the Holy Spirit wants to reveal to you. *Respond in your journal.*

Part Four

Finding Your Fit

Many Christians are disjointed and aimless because they have no pattern before them after which conduct and character are to be shaped. They just move aimlessly, their minds in a cloudy state, no pattern in view, no point in sight, no standard after which they are striving. There is no standard by which to value and gauge their efforts. No magnet is there to fill their eyes, quicken their steps, draw them, and keep them steady.

—E. M. Bounds[1]

Divine Design

WHEN I WAS working as the Director of Servant Ministries, we developed a workshop to assess a believer's "divine design," to help church members find their best ministry fit. Though the assessments are helpful, they are only tools, not adequate replacements for the leading of the Holy Spirit or a humble willingness to serve occasionally where there is a need. I think the assessments may be most effective in helping us sense what is not a good ministry fit. Let me share an example.

When our grandson was three years old, I got a call from the children's Sunday school director, asking if I would serve in Zachary's preschool class the following Sunday since the regular teacher would be out of town. Sure! No problem. How difficult can it be?

I spent the next week preparing for a ninety-minute lesson. I know that those of you who work in the preschool department are having a good laugh at my ignorance. That's OK, go ahead and laugh. It really is rather humorous. I will tell you that when I arrived and waited patiently for my fifteen three-year-olds, I was more nervous and intimidated than if I were about to speak at a national conference of a thousand adults.

The morning got off to a chaotic start, and I knew very quickly that I was not in control. I finished my ninety-minute lesson in less than fifteen minutes, with only two little girls paying any attention at all. I had over an hour yet to go, and I would have paid any price to bring in someone who knew what we were supposed to be doing. At the end of class, I was totally drained of all energy. I think it was a fairly good indication that I was not called to minister to young children. What do you think?

Let's look at what the Word says about our unique design and call to serve.

For you created my inmost being; you knit me together in my mother's womb. I praise you because I am fearfully and wonderfully made; your works are wonderful, I know that full well.

—Psalm 139:13–14

For we are God's workmanship, created in Christ Jesus to do good works, which God prepared in advance for us to do.

—Ephesians 2:10

Now to each one the manifestation of the Spirit is given for the common good.

—1 Corinthians 12:7

It was he who gave some to be apostles, some to be prophets, some to be evangelists, and some to be pastors and teachers, to prepare God's people for works of service, so that the body of Christ may be built up until we all reach unity in the faith and in the knowledge of the Son of God and become mature, attaining to the whole measure of the fullness of Christ.

—Ephesians 4:11–13

This service that you perform is not only supplying the needs of God's people but is also overflowing in many expressions of thanks to God.

—2 Corinthians 9:12

Let's summarize. We are God's workmanship, wonderfully created for good works in order to:

- Serve the common good.
- Build up the body of Christ.
- Reach unity in the faith.
- Become mature.
- Serve the needs of God's people.
- Give thanks to God.

Let's begin with a look at your personality.

PERSONALITY

Far too many times over the years, I have made excuses for my blunt, hurtful comments or my controlling behavior by simply saying, "Well, it's just the way I am—part of my personality." The way we use the word "personality" in everyday language suggests we are talking about the combination of our *temperament* and our *character*.

Temperament

Our temperament is inborn, part of our DNA. No matter how long we are on the journey with Christ, our temperament will not really change. Social scientists have studied human behavior for thousands of years. Hippocrates was the first to describe four basic temperaments. This was 400 years before the birth of Christ. He called them choleric, sanguine, melancholic, and phlegmatic. Over time they have been called by many other names, but the descriptions have remained amazingly reliable over the centuries.

We can identify the four temperaments rather quickly by asking two simple questions: First, are you an extrovert or an introvert? Second, are you task-oriented or people-oriented? We can place these four temperaments on a grid. The horizontal line separates the extroverts from the introverts, and the vertical line separates the task-oriented types from the people-oriented types.

Task-oriented Extrovert	**People-oriented Extrovert**
Task-oriented Introvert	**People-oriented Introvert**

Dr. John Trent is a Christian author and counselor who created a personality tool called **The LOBG Personal Strengths Survey** that refers to the four temperaments as Lion, Otter, Golden Retriever and Beaver. This tool is found in the book he wrote with his friend and another well known Christian author, Gary Smalley, called *The Two Sides of Love*, Focus on the Family Publishers, 2008. I like this tool because it is user friendly, quick to administer, and lists only the strengths of each temperament type. Each description presents a positive image of the God-given traits for that group.

"The LOBG Personal Strengths Assessment"®
Used with permission, Dr. John Trent, 2011

Lion

Takes charge	Bold
Determined	Purposeful
Assertive	Decision maker
Firm	Leader
Enterprising	Goal-driven
Competitive	Self-reliant
Enjoys challenge	Adventurous

"Let's do it now!"

Double the number circled_____

Otter

Takes risks	Fun loving
Visionary	Likes variety
Motivator	Enjoys change
Energetic	Creative
Very verbal	Group-oriented
Promoter	Mixes easily
Avoids details	Optimistic

"Trust me! It'll work out!"

Double the number circled_____

Beaver

Deliberate	Discerning
Controlled	Detailed
Reserved	Analytical
Predictable	Inquisitive
Practical	Precise
Orderly	Persistent
Factual	Scheduled

"How was it done in the past?"

Double the number circled _____

Golden Retriever

Loyal	Adaptable
Nondemanding	Sympathetic
Even keel	Thoughtful
Avoids conflict	Nurturing
Enjoys routine	Patient
Dislikes change	Tolerant
Deep relationships	Good listener

"Let's keep things the way they are."

Double the number circled _____

Directions: In each of the four quadrants, circle all the traits that you believe are typical of you, including the quote. Count the total number of circles in each quadrant and double the number, which is your score for that quadrant. Most people will have a dominant temperament and a secondary one. There are a few people who will score equally across all four quadrants, but this is a rare exception.

In Relationships

Once you know someone's temperament, you can predict how he or she might respond to any given situation. Let me use my sister and myself as an example. I am a Lion/Otter. I love being with people. I am energized by them. As I write this chapter, I am sitting in a small mountain cottage with no one around, no cell phone service, no TV, and no radio reception, except a country music station that is mostly static. The sole purpose for coming was to get away from all distractions at home so I could finish this book. I've been here for several weeks, and it almost feels like punishment. As a believer, I should probably think of it as a sacrifice. I am ready to head back to my very busy, people-filled life in town. When I get home, I will need to be around people to re-energize; right now, I am borderline comatose.

My sister is a very high scoring Beaver. She would sacrifice almost anything to have a few weeks alone in a mountain cottage, as long as she had her computer and Internet access so she could spend her days researching. She would go home very refreshed indeed. Neither reaction is good or bad, just predictable.

Understanding these fundamental differences is crucial to healthy relationships. It is particularly important in marriage, the most intimate human union. My husband is a Beaver. He likes order and predictability. He takes a long time to make a decision, to be sure he has all the information he needs. I enjoy spontaneity, variety, and am more likely to make rapid, gut-level decisions that may seem impulsive to him. If I have something to discuss with him, I can't do so just because it has popped into my head at the moment. I need to be sensitive to his schedule. So I'll say something like, "Would you have some time tonight to discuss a few things?"

He might say, "Can it wait? I had hoped to get caught up on some paperwork tonight." As a people-oriented person, I can't even imagine putting off a discussion in order to do paperwork. It is beyond my comprehension. But if I pushed to have that discussion right then and there, he would have been frustrated and under stress. As a task-oriented person who needs predictability, he already had his evening plotted and planned.

If it were really important, I might say, "Can you juggle your schedule a bit tonight because we have something important to discuss?" When you understand how someone is likely to respond to a given situation, you can choose to make adjustments that promote harmony instead of expecting him to respond as you would and then getting angry when he doesn't.

My daughter is a high-scoring Otter, whose core value is fun. She is always the life of the party and can be counted on to provide stories, games, and loads of laughter. And she is usually late. I used to get so angry at her for being late all the time, but I now understand that Otters are not time-focused but event-focused. The event will start for her when she arrives. So I don't ask her to bring the appetizers for the Thanksgiving meal. Dessert is the better option. When we fail to understand someone's temperament, we often set that person up for failure and then punish her when she fails. We criticize and complain because she did not respond as we would have responded.

Character

Now let's understand the difference between temperament and character. Traits of temperament are morally neutral; they are not good or bad. Character, on the other hand, has more to do with morality. Let's look at the Lion's trait of boldness. *Boldness* is morally neutral. *Brashness*, on the other hand, is morally negative. It implies that someone is self-assertive in an aggressive or rude way. Boldness is a trait of the temperament, brashness is a character flaw, part of our human sin nature. Character flaws diminish as we grow in Christlikeness.

As a Lion, I always will have some element of boldness, but as a maturing disciple of Christ, brashness is no longer part of my character. The Spirit of Christ in me purifies and prunes away the character flaws but leaves my God-given temperament intact. This is critical to your understanding of who you were created to be.

Action steps: Complete the Personal Strength Survey. After determining your primary and secondary strengths, create a list of all the personality weaknesses you can identify in yourself. Delete all those that are morally neutral and review what is left.

Reflection question: In your relationships at home, at work, or in the church, what struggles can you identify that may be due to differences in temperament? Which ones are more likely due to issues of character?

Prayer: Spend time in prayer, reflecting and receiving what the Holy Spirit wants to reveal to you. *Respond in your journal.*

Chapter 23

Clarifying Your Personal Values

SEVERAL YEARS AGO, I was presenting an idea for a creative writing project for our mission school in Zambia. I proposed a writing competition among the students in the ninth grade, the highest level at the school. Though all the entries would be included in the book we were creating, the student with the winning entry would be invited to spend a weekend at a small tourist lodge in a nearby town, a very rare opportunity. There appeared to be no enthusiasm for the project among the teachers and the administration. Not wanting to hurt my feelings with the truth, they just tabled the decision for a later time.

That evening, I shared my surprise with one of the more "seasoned" missionaries and discovered that it was simply a conflict of values. In the North American culture, we *value* competition, especially when there is a prize attached. In much of Africa, the value is collaboration. And what about the prize? No one would want to be singled out for special treatment. It would generate envy and separation, to be avoided at all costs in a culture that values community so highly. It was a great life lesson in the importance of values.

As you proceed to find your "fit" for ministry, it is important to clarify your personal values, as they will help you make decisions that enable you to live authentically. It is possible to have a different set of values for different sectors of your life. Here are some examples:

As a parent, my list of values (after unconditional love) might be:

- Availability
- Consistency

- Encouragement
- Humor
- Prayer

As a Christian coach, my list might look like this:

- Authenticity
- Accountability
- Competency
- Confidentiality
- Prayer
- Trust

In my role as a wife:

- Intimacy
- Commitment
- Honesty
- Honor
- Prayer
- Respect

These values guide the decisions I make in each of the roles I serve. But there is another set of values, called *core values*, which are more fundamental and will be the overriding values that carry into every area of my life.

WHAT IS A CORE VALUE?

At its most basic, a core value is a concept, conviction, or character trait that defines what you care about most—the essence of what is most important to you. Core values are the non-negotiable, deeply-rooted elements that determine what you stand for. If they are "core," you should be living them now, not some time in the future. Jack Lannon, in his book *Untapped Potential*, writes, "We will be an outliving expression of these in living core values."[1] They are not your goals or dreams and are not to be confused with your passions, though many lists of values include what I would consider a passion. Values are generally abstract concepts, rather than concrete things. For example:

- Value: Patriotism
- Passion: United States of America

- Value: Discipleship
- Passion: Women

- Value: Truth
- Passion: Writing (We will explore passion in a later chapter.)

As biblical Christians, most of us value faith, family, and friendship. Beyond that, your list of core values may be very different from mine or that of any other person in your circle of friends. It will be unique to you. Most of us, however, go through life without ever clarifying our core values, and yet they are often the root of disharmony in marriages, careers, or ministries. The authors of *Discover Who You Are* provide this simple, but charming example:

> Being in charge of the children's Christmas program, for example, may fit your life gifts for creativity and management, your spiritual gifts of leadership and administration, and your passion for children's ministry—*but* if you value accuracy and control, you will be doomed to frustration as the "little lambs" wander off and the Wise Men forget to carry their gifts to the manger.[2]

At times, we need to set aside our own values for the sake of unity, but when we have to compromise a core value, it can cause stress and disharmony. If there is not a shared set of core values in marriage, it can lead to dissention and, ultimately, to divorce. For example, if the wife has a core value of security, and the husband is an entrepreneur who enjoys the thrill of risk, she may live a life of stress, disappointment, and distrust. Their core values are in direct opposition.

Here's an example from my own life. One of my core values is authenticity. But I live in the South, where a strong cultural value is graciousness. I am always trying to figure out how to be real *and* gracious. In the past, I often failed miserably because I could not "fake it." It just goes against my "core."

A biblical value, however, should always trump a personal core value. The more mature we are in the faith and the more we submit to the Spirit, the easier this will become. In Romans 12:18, Paul tells us, "If it is possible, as far as it depends on you, live at peace with everyone." If my core value of authenticity will cause misunderstanding or division, I will choose the higher biblical value of peace.

Action step: Review the values listed in the chart on pages 123–124. Circle all that seem to define what you value. Then review your list and delete those that, though they may be important, are not necessarily your core values. Try to narrow it down to about six. *Faith, family,* and *friends* are assumed, so select six others. The values mentioned here are just examples, so please add as many as you need to identify six values that are most important to you. Then write a short statement of what each value means in your life—what it looks like when you are living it out. Here are several examples:

- Value: Authenticity
- Living it: I live in open, honest vulnerability with nothing to hide, nothing to prove, and nothing to lose.

- Value: Simplicity
- Living it: I choose to live simply that others might simply live, avoiding extravagant spending, materialistic living, and restless doing.

Reflection question: Having identified your core values, are there any previous ministry experiences that have been unfulfilling or ineffective due to a "misalignment" with your core values?

Prayer: Spend time in prayer, reflecting and receiving what the Holy Spirit wants to reveal to you. *Respond in your journal.*

Core Values

acceptance	confidentiality	fairness	honor
accountability	conformity	faith	hospitality
accuracy	consensus	faithfulness	humor
achievement	consistency	family	independence
advancement	control	fantasy	individuality
adventure	convenience	fasting	industriousness
aesthetics	cooperation	fellowship	influence
affirmation	creativity	financial security	integrity
affluence	critical-thinking	fitness	intellegence
appreciation	determination	flexibility	interdependence
authenticity	devotion	formal	intimacy
balance	diligence	freedom	justice
beauty	discernment	friendship	kindness
benevolence	discipleship	frugality	knowledge
biblical truth	discretion	fun	laughter
caution	diversity	generosity	leadership
challenge	dreams	gentleness	learning
change	duty	grace	legacy
character	efficiency	gratitude	leisure
choice	emotion	growth	liberty
clarity	empowerment	happiness	life
collaboration	encouragement	harmony	longevity
comfort	energy	healing	love
commitment	enterprise	health	loyalty
communication	entrepreneurship	heritage	marriage
community	environment	heritage	materialism
compassion	evangelism	heroism	maturity
competence	excellence	holiness	memories
competition	exploration	home	mercy
compromise	expression	honesty	missions

motivation	privacy	solidarity	wholeness
music	productivity	solitude	wilderness
nature	professionalism	spontaneity	wisdom
negotiation	profit	stability	wonder
nurture	promise	stewardship	work
obedience	promptness	strength	worship
opportunity	prosperity	submission	
order	protection	success	
organization	prudence	surprise	
originality	purpose	surrender	
parenthood	quality	synergy	
passion	quiet	team work	
paternalism	recognition	tenacity	
patience	reconciliation	thriftiness	
patriotism	recreation	tolerance	
peace	reflection	tradition	
performance	relationship	transformation	
persistence	reliability	transparency	
personal development	responsibility	travel	
physical fitness	restoration	trust	
poise	romance	truth	
possessions	routine	uniqueness	
potential	Sabbath	unity	
power	sacrifice	valor	
practicality	security	variety	
praise	self-control	versatility	
prayer	sensitivity	victory	
precision	service	vitality	
prestige	simplicity	wealth	
pride	sincerity	wellness	

The Desires of Our Hearts

PASSION IS IGNITED in so many different ways. Now, of course, I am *not* referring to the romantic kind of passion; I am referring to the kind that energizes you with vibrant purpose. It is that *"something"* that will get you up and out the door when there is no money to be made or personal recognition to be gained. And it is not a golf game, a shopping spree, or any other personal pleasure. It is something beyond yourself. When you can identify it, it will often be a clue to your ministry or your life purpose.

Sometimes God calls you into a ministry for which you have absolutely no passion. That was the case when He called me into women's ministry. But once I knew beyond a doubt that He was calling me down that path, I also knew I could not do it without passion. So it became the focus of my prayer life. And He was faithful to answer my prayers.

Other times, passion is born out of life experiences. Some of the most effective ministries are birthed from a passion that has emerged out of our greatest pain. My sister-in-law, a victim of child sexual abuse, leads a recovery ministry for other victims. Sybil, a precious sister in Christ, launched a prayer ministry called Mothers of Prodigals after years of praying for her own prodigal to come home. They meet monthly for prayer, fellowship, and encouragement. Who better to "weep with those who weep" and offer the gift of hope?

Let me share a story from my own passion profile. When our son, Geoff, was two years old, he still hadn't spoken his first word. By three he had developed a rather charming sign language, and along with grunting and pointing, he made himself understood, at least by the family. Geoff was later diagnosed with dyslexia, and by fifth grade, he still couldn't read beyond a first grade level. We sent him to a private school for children with learning disabilities, but a year later, he had made no significant progress. We contacted the medical university in a nearby town that had a dyslexia research program. They said he would need one-on-one tutoring for three to five hours a day at the cost of $110 per hour. Well, that was not sustainable! I began to pray fervently for direction. "Lord, what are we going to do? Who can we get to help him?"

He answered, but it was not the answer I was looking for. He said, "You will."

"Lord, what do I know about teaching dyslexic children? I have finally finished graduate school, and, well, I had a different plan." But His Spirit had clearly spoken to my spirit, so I began the process of learning all I could about reading disabilities and the teaching techniques that would help.

The following fall, we pulled Geoff out of school and set up our official home school for the start of sixth grade. That first year, I eliminated everything from his curriculum except language arts and math. We spent five hours a day in language study and one hour on math.

That first semester was unbelievable and, at times, unbearable. Only two things got me through: first, knowing it was God's will and, second, *not* having the gift of compassion. If I had had a strong compassion gift, I would have given in as he cried, begged, and stomped up the stairs to his room in defeat. Instead, I set the timer for twenty minutes and told him to have a good cry, and I would be up to get him when the timer "dinged." He was so convinced that he never would learn to read that he felt like I was punishing him for hours and hours a day. I began to fear that our relationship would be forever damaged.

I told him, "God would not have sent us down this path if there was no hope. Trust me, you will learn to read. If you work hard for six hours a day, I will give you no homework or projects to do after school. And I promise *never* to give you busy work."

It was still a struggle, but by the end of the semester, he was beginning to sound out fourth grade words. He began to believe it was possible. I saw my son awaken to the excitement of new possibilities. We continued to home school until he was sixteen, and then we sent him off to community college. He later transferred to the university and graduated with a degree in Business Administration. As I write this chapter, Geoff is running for a seat on the City Council, and he recently has begun to talk about going back to school for an MBA. To God be the glory, great things He has done!

Now I have a passion for adult illiteracy! I am tutoring Walt, an adult dyslexic, who, in his forty-one years, never has learned to read. When I finish this book, I hope to launch a tutor training program for our community outreach ministry. Next to the gift of knowing Christ, I can't think of a greater blessing than giving the gift of literacy.

Recently, I bought a Bible for Walt, a beautiful black leather one. He now can read the opening words of the gospel of John for himself: "In the beginning was the Word, and the Word was with God, and the Word was God. He was with God in the beginning" (John 1:1–2).

CLARIFYING YOUR PASSION

Your passion may be for a particular cause, like homelessness or hunger, or for a segment of the population, like single mothers or at-risk youth. Of course, these examples could go on and on.

Have you ever sensed God stirring your heart for something beyond yourself, perhaps something that seems outlandish or even impossible? Or has He prepared you for something through your life experiences that points the way to your purpose? You might ask, "Is there only one purpose for my life?" I would say not. There are seasons of life, and each may bring with it a new direction. I believe that the key is obedience. How faithful are we to the first stirring?

In the parable of the talents, Christ tells the first and second servants, "Well done, good and faithful servant! You have been faithful with a few things; I will put you in charge of many things. Come and share your Master's happiness!" (Matt. 25:21–23). John Avant, author of the *Passion Promise*, writes, "You are designed for a life of passion—a life only God can imagine."[1]

Action step: Review your life story cards, and see if you can discover a trend toward a particular cause, or perhaps an experience that once stirred your soul. Then begin to list a few of those things that ignite a passion in you.

Reflection question: If time or money were not limiting factors, what would compel you out the door and into service?

Prayer: Spend time in prayer, reflecting and receiving what the Holy Spirit wants to reveal to you. *Respond in your journal.*

Doing What Comes Naturally

WE KNEW IT when he was only two years old. Our grandson had natural athletic abilities! Ken bought Zachary a small, plastic baseball bat and ball and took him to the backyard to show him how to hit. Ken thought it would be a great way to spend time with Zachary that would not require him to roll around on the floor, something he does not do so well. Zachary seemed to need no instruction. Ken pitched, and Zachary hit, sending granddad into the street to chase ball after ball. His hand-eye coordination was astounding. Since that time, Zachary has excelled at most every sport he has attempted. Without a doubt, it is simply God-given ability. I pray he uses it to glorify God and serve His kingdom purposes.

The body of Christ is an amazing mosaic of natural talents, skills, and experiences that could be used for advancing the kingdom, promoting the church, meeting human needs, and bringing glory to God. Sadly, however, we often compartmentalize those abilities, enjoying them in our secular life and never thinking of them as potential ministry gifts. Let's look at a few examples of those who have understood the eternal value of those gifts:

- A young man who is a gifted athlete now uses his talent in an inner-city soccer ministry with at-risk youth.
- A young woman with a creative gift and a well-developed skill in photography serves on the technical team of the church, creating videos for Sunday services.
- A small team of men—a plumber, electrician, and carpenter—service the homes of single mothers in the congregation and the community.

The stories could go on and on, for there is no lack of ability in the body of Christ. The problem is a segmented framework that labels some things as secular and some as spiritual. Since I am a disciple of Christ, everything belongs to the Lord. Remember the parable of the talents (Matt. 25:14–30)? We are to invest what we have been given to expand the Master's kingdom and to bring Him glory.

Action step: Create a list of all your abilities. Include natural talents, skills, and experiences. Begin to let your imagination run free, and identify at least three abilities that could be used in ministry.

Reflection question: In the past, what abilities have you considered purely secular?

Prayer: Spend time in prayer, reflecting and receiving what the Holy Spirit wants to reveal to you. *Respond in your journal.*

Gifted by God

BECAUSE OF THE controversy surrounding the issue of spiritual gifts, I am somewhat reluctant to address it. But the gifts are biblical, powerful, and essential in fulfilling our roles as advocates for the church and activists in the community. Bible teacher and author Kenneth Boa describes two different views: Word-centered believers think that the gifts of tongues, healing, and prophesy, called sign gifts, gradually disappeared from the church once the New Testament canon was complete. Spirit-centered believers think that all the gifts are still given.[1]

Let me state from the beginning that I do not come from a charismatic tradition and have not been given the gift of tongues, healing, or prophesy. On the other hand, two very dear friends of mine, neither of whom was raised in the charismatic tradition, have been given the gift of tongues; they just don't demonstrate this gift in our church. I am of the opinion that God can give whatever gift He chooses to whomever He chooses whenever He chooses to give it.

Even in the early days of the church, the gift of tongues created controversy. The apostle Paul said to the church at Corinth: "Now, brothers, if I come to you and speak in tongues, what good will I be to you, unless I bring you some revelation or knowledge or prophesy or word of instruction? . . . Since you are eager to have spiritual gifts, try to excel in gifts that build up the church (1 Cor. 14:6, 12).

Most of the verses that identify spiritual gifts are found in Romans 12:4–8; 1 Corinthians 12:1–31; and Ephesians 4:11–13. Here is a brief summary of them adapted from the website www.mintools.com, an online source for ministry tools and resources.

- Administration—the gift of organization and management
- Apostleship—the gift to pioneer new churches or ministries
- Discernment—the gift to detect the spirit of truth from that of error

- Evangelism—the gift to lead unbelievers to a saving knowledge of Christ
- Exhortation—the gift to motivate someone through words of counsel or encouragement
- Faith—the gift to believe that God's plans will be accomplished regardless of the apparent circumstances
- Giving—the gift to contribute material resources generously and cheerfully
- Healing—the gift to be used by God as a channel for physical, emotional, and spiritual healing
- Helps—the gift to serve the needs of another to enhance his or her ministry
- Interpretation of tongues—the gift to translate the words spoken in tongues into the common language of the people
- Knowledge—the gift to gather and analyze biblical information in a systematic way for the benefit of others
- Leadership—the gift to discern God's purpose for a group and to communicate the goals and motivate others to get involved in order to accomplish the work
- Mercy—the gift to empathize and engage in ministries of compassion to serve those in need
- Miracles—the gift to be used by God to accomplish the supernatural
- Pastor—the gift to spiritually lead, nourish, protect, and care for a group of believers
- Prophecy—the gift to receive and proclaim a message from God
- Service—the gift to identify tasks that need doing and gather the necessary materials to accomplish the tasks
- Teaching—the gift to clearly explain God's Word so others may learn
- Tongues—the gift of a private "prayer language" or the public use of tongues, which must be interpreted for the church to be edified
- Wisdom—the gift to apply the Word of God in practical ways

Authors Don and Katie Fortune divide the spiritual gifts into three categories:

1. Manifestation gifts, like healing and miracles, are a manifestation of the Holy Spirit's working through someone. No one can dictate how, when, or where these gifts will be used. Only the Holy Spirit determines the use of these gifts.[3]
2. Ministry gifts are those listed in Ephesians 4, referring to people "who were called and gifted to lead and train the rest of the body of Christ."[4] Some examples are apostles, evangelists, pastors, and teachers.
3. Motivational gifts, like exhortation, mercy, or service, can be the motivating force for our lives and ministries.[5]

Discovering your spiritual gifts can be another clue to the plan and purpose that God has for your life and ministry. If you never have taken a spiritual gifts assessment, there are several online versions, some available for a small fee, a few free of charge. I found the website www.mintools.com to be helpful.

Action step: Complete a spiritual gifts assessment.

Reflection question: What is the value of knowing your spiritual gifts?

Prayer: Spend time in prayer, reflecting and receiving what the Holy Spirit wants to reveal to you. *Respond in your journal.*

Seeking a New Vision

IN MY LAST semester of coach training, I worked with a young Christian woman who was living a defeated life. She was entrenched in an unhealthy marriage, deeply in debt, overworked, overweight, and overwhelmed. She constantly fought fatigue and felt guilty about her failure to spend quality time with her children. She still was haunted by an abusive past and hung on to distorted lies of the enemy. Every day was drudgery; and even sleep brought no real rest.

Together we worked through many of the issues and action steps presented in this book. Then I suggested she spend time alone with the Lord, asking for a *vision* of what life could look like if she were living in *authentic faith*, in harmony with Him. She questioned if life could ever be different.

In his book *The Dream Releasers*, Wayne Cordeiro writes:

In every life is contained all the potential through which God can accomplish great things. . . . Regardless of what you see, remember that the master designer is not finished. You might not be able to see the classic lines of a masterpiece, but the potential for greatness is there. . . . When the Hebrews saw Moses as a selfish murderer, God saw the message-bearer for the books of Genesis, Exodus, Leviticus, Numbers and Deuteronomy. When others saw Peter as a rash, impulsive fisherman, God saw the rock upon which He would build His church.[1]

But how do you begin to pursue the vision? Intentionally!

SMART Goals

Business consultants and life coaches often have used the SMART goal format to help clients focus their efforts and increase their likelihood of achieving their goals. SMART is an acronym that stands for Specific, Measurable, Achievable, Relevant, and Time sensitive. It's all about being intentional. Most people wander through life living in default mode, simply responding to the circumstances that confront them every day. As Disciples of Christ, we have a God-designed purpose. "For we are God's workmanship, created in Christ Jesus to do good works, which God prepared in advance for us to do" (Eph. 2:10).

Let's look at a few examples of goal statements.

1. "I want to be a better student of the Bible." This is an important goal, but it is not a SMART goal. It is too vague and has no measurable outcome or time limit. How will you know when you have achieved this?
2. "I want to read through the whole Bible this year." This is not yet a SMART goal. Though it is specific, it reads more like a desire than a plan of action.
3. "I will read the gospel of John, at least one chapter a day, at least five days a week, and complete it in four weeks." Now that is a SMART goal.

   ▪ It is very specific. You know exactly what you are going to do.
   ▪ It is measurable—at least one chapter a day, at least five days a week.
   ▪ It is likely attainable because the gospel of John has only twenty-one chapters.
   ▪ It is relevant to your desire to become a better student of the Bible.
   ▪ It is time-sensitive. You will know that you have achieved it or not achieved it at the end of four weeks.

Does this seem rather artificial and rigid to you? Those of you who prefer routine are probably loving it. But I'm sure that those of you who prefer a more free and flexible lifestyle are less than enthusiastic. You are the very group who will benefit the most from some intentional goal-setting. So don't overlook this effective tool. It is only a tool, not a rule.

Remember, regardless of your temperament, God has work for you to do. Goal-setting is simply a chapter in your servant training manual that will help you live your life on purpose—His purpose.

In the next chapter, you will decide where you will begin. You will develop a SMART goal to increase the likelihood that you will see transformation, taking you a step closer to your new vision.

Action step: Just for practice, select one area in your life you would like to improve. Create a goal for yourself. Be sure that it is a SMART goal: specific, measurable, achievable, relevant, and time sensitive.

Reflection question: Reflect on a time when you attempted to change a behavior or attain a goal. How successful were you? How would a SMART goal have changed the way you worked toward that goal?

Prayer: Spend time in prayer, reflecting and receiving what the Holy Spirit wants to reveal to you. *Respond in your journal.*

Living with Purpose

EVERY ONE OF us will end up somewhere, but few of us will end up there on purpose. Most of us live in "default" mode—reactive rather than proactive. Most never will experience all that God has planned for them. Chuck Swindoll wrote, "Mediocrity is fast becoming the by-word of our times. . . . Why live differently in a society where it's so much easier to look the same and swim downstream? . . . It is my firm conviction that those who impact and reshape the world are the ones committed to living above the level of mediocrity."[1]

Living as an authentic disciple of Christ means becoming more and more conformed to His image and no longer being conformed to the pattern of this world (Rom.12:2). We can enhance this process of transformation by living intentionally. I encourage you to do an honest self-assessment. Even Scripture calls us to examine ourselves: "Examine yourselves to see whether you are in the faith; test yourselves. Do you not realize that Christ Jesus is in you—unless, of course, you fail the test?" (2 Cor. 13:5).

Once you have completed your assessment, I will ask you to determine what your next step will be and to create a SMART goal that will move you closer to following in the Master's footsteps. It is best that you select only one area to begin with. Research shows that you dramatically decrease your probability of success when you focus on more than one area at a time. You can continue to return to this book again and again, like a training manual, as you make the decision to "live above the level of mediocrity." And I pray, ". . . that by his power he may fulfill every good purpose of yours and every act prompted by your faith" (2 Thess. 1:11b).

Self-Assessment

Taking off the Old Self

Answer the following questions on a scale of 1 to 10, with 10 being the highest level of agreement.

- I have fully surrendered all beliefs and attitudes that compete with a biblical worldview.

  Strongly disagree   1   2   3   4   5   6   7   8   9   10   Strongly agree

- I no longer dwell on the past and have forgiven completely those who have wounded me.

  Strongly disagree   1   2   3   4   5   6   7   8   9   10   Strongly agree

- I want nothing more than I want intimacy with Christ and will graciously surrender all that I have as He directs.

  Strongly disagree   1   2   3   4   5   6   7   8   9   10   Strongly agree

- I have surrendered my right to rule over my life. Christ now sits in the seat of authority over my will.

  Strongly disagree   1   2   3   4   5   6   7   8   9   10   Strongly agree

If you honestly know that you are not fully surrendered, this may be where you focus your efforts. What will it take for you finally to say, "I have been crucified with Christ and I no longer live, but Christ lives in me"?

Putting on the New Self

For each of the following "habits in pursuit of holiness" discussed in Chapter 17, create a vision of what that habit would look like in your life if you were seeking to draw closer to Christ and live a life of greater devotion. (Respond in your journal.)

- In the Word
- In prayer
- In worship
- In service

FINDING YOUR FIT

Summarize your findings here:

- Personal Strength Survey (Chapter 22)

  Primary temperament

  _____

  Secondary temperament

  _____

- Core Values (Chapter 23)

  _____   _____

  _____   _____

  _____   _____

- Passions (Chapter 24)

  _____

  _____

  _____

- Abilities (Chapter 25)

  _____   _____

  _____   _____

  _____   _____

- Spiritual gifts (Chapter 26)

  _____

  _____

  _____

Bearing Much Fruit

Now that you have reviewed your "divine design," prayerfully consider how God has prepared you to serve as an ambassador of Christ, an advocate for the church, and an activist in the community.

Action steps (select one to begin):

○ What do you still need to surrender in order to take off the old self? Is it your worldview, your wounds, your wants, or your will? Select one area to focus on, and create a SMART goal to define your next step. Then share it with an accountability partner.

○ What habits do you need to cultivate in order to put on the new self? Is it in the area of studying the Word, prayer, worship, or service? Select one area to focus on, and create a SMART goal that will move you closer to your "new self." Then share it with an accountability partner.

○ How will you live out your roles as an ambassador of Christ, an advocate for the church, and an activist in your community? Select an area to focus on, and create a SMART goal to move you in that direction. Then share it with an accountability partner.

Reflection question: What are some stumbling blocks that you see ahead that might keep you from achieving your goal? What proactive steps can you take to prevent them from hindering your progress?

Prayer: Spend time in prayer, reflecting and receiving what the Holy Spirit wants to reveal to you. *Respond in your journal.*

Following Your New Path

THE PURSUIT OF authentic faith and abundant life is never a solo journey. For me, there is a long list of people who have left their gentle footprints on my soul. Their legacy has led me to the "narrow gate" (Matt. 7:13). But choosing to walk through that gate, a passage from death to life, is a personal commitment to surrender anything and everything that challenges the sovereignty and authority of Christ as King. When you walk through that gate, you surrender your "rights." You have become a servant of the Most High God, filled to the measure of all the fullness of Christ. Anne Graham Lotz described it well in her book *I Saw the Lord*:

> To be filled with His Spirit is to be moment-by-moment surrendered to His moment-by-moment control in my life. The result is that I am increasingly His look-alike and His act-alike and His live-alike. It means that the beautiful facets of His glorious nature—His love and His joy and His peace and His patience and His kindness and His goodness and His faithfulness and His gentleness and His self-control—are more and more obvious in my life, obvious even to those who know me best and live closest to me and work side by side with me.[1]

She goes on to say, "If Jesus could turn the world upside down with twelve disciples who were filled with the Holy Spirit, can you imagine what He could do today if every person who claims to be born again into God's family were filled with the Spirit?!"[2] Imagine it indeed! Then accept His invitation to die! And take your place in the kingdom—a workman who need not be ashamed (2 Tim. 2:15).

I would love to hear from you as you pursue Christ with your whole heart, mind, soul, and strength. I would consider it a privilege and a blessing if you would share your struggles, your doubts, and most especially, your victories. And I can't wait to meet with you in eternity. I wonder if there will be celestial coffee shops, perhaps with golden bistro tables? It seems I have had the best spiritual conversations over coffee.

Let me close with the words of the child of God from the Parable of Living Water: "Father, it is beyond words! I am filled to the measure of all the fullness of Christ. And it is more than I ever could have hoped for or imagined; my weakness for His strength, my depravity for His divinity, my poverty for His provision, my arrogance for His humility, my wounds for His healing, and my death for His life."

Amen!

Author's contact information:
E-mail: mshullnc@gmail.com
Website: MarieShull.com

Coaching Principles and Practices

GEORGE BARNA, THE Christian researcher and author, says that believers in Christ are not much different from nonbelievers in how they think and live.[1] He writes, ". . . most born-again adults are limited in their ability to grow spiritually because they have failed to set any goals for their spiritual development, failed to develop standards against which to measure their growth, or failed to establish procedures for being held accountable for their growth."[2]

Spiritual growth rarely occurs in isolation. The body of Christ was not meant to function that way. What Barna has described above is the role of a coach, someone to help you set goals, measure your progress, and hold you accountable.

When you think of a coach, you may have the typical image of a whistle-blowing, hard-driving, vein-bulging, screaming man in a warm-up suit. When I speak of a coach, I refer to a *discipleship coach*, which I will call simply "the coach" for brevity.

How does a coach differ from a counselor or a mentor?

- A counselor's focus is mainly on the past. She helps a client deal with old wounds, encourages forgiveness, and works toward emotional wellness.
- A mentor's focus is mainly on the present. She may be someone who has more life experience and who freely shares what God has done in her life and may offer biblical wisdom for dealing with life issues.
- A coach's focus is mainly on the future. She will ask powerful questions, practice effective listening, help you establish goals and action steps, encourage your efforts, and hold you accountable. A coach's primary goal is to be a catalyst for change, but she never gives advice, judges your decisions, or takes responsibility for your choices.

I invite you to become a coach for someone in your small group or in a one-on-one relationship as you work though the process of "taking off the old self" and "putting on the new self." As a coach, you will be actively engaged in discussions that reflect on the past, even though that will not be your focus, so just a few words of caution. If you sense there are deep, unresolved wounds of the past that are not confessed, forgiven, and surrendered after responding to the suggested exercises and intense prayer, suggest to your coaching partner that she seek the help of a Spirit-filled Christian counselor. It is the one time you are encouraged to give advice, but remember that you are not responsible for her decision.

Allow me to begin with some basic *coaching concepts*.

1. *God is at work in the life of a believer* (Phil. 1:6). You are not responsible for the spiritual growth of your partner. It is the Holy Spirit's role to convict and conform her to the image of Christ and to bear fruit in her life. Richard Foster, in *Celebration of Discipline*, says, ". . . we must come to the place in our lives where we can lay down the everlasting burden of always needing to manage others. . . . When we genuinely believe that inner transformation is God's work and not ours, we can put to rest our passion to set others straight."[3]

2. *The foundation of coaching is authenticity.* If you must protect your image by glossing over your faults and minimizing your failures, you will have difficulty taking off the mask of perfection and allowing your coaching partner to be "real" with you.

3. *The hallmark of a coaching relationship is confidentiality.* You must create a safe place for your coaching partner to share her most private struggles without any fear that you will share the information with others—even disguised as a prayer request.

4. *Coaching involves asking, not telling.* As a coaching partner, you can have a conversation that lasts several hours and never give a single piece of advice. Coaching involves asking a question, listening intuitively, and then responding with another question.

5. *Coaching requires no agenda for the partner.* Even if you see a glaring issue that needs to be addressed, do not assume the Holy Spirit is ready to reveal it to your coaching partner. If you attempt to reveal it before the Spirit has prepared the way, you will encounter resistance and perhaps rejection. That's why intuitive listening is so important. We'll talk more about listening in Coaching Conversations, Appendix 2.

6. *Judging or criticizing has no place in a coaching relationship.* Once you truly release *all* control over your partner's choices, it is much easier to overcome a judging or critical spirit. This is not to suggest that you give up being concerned, but that you give up trying to be the Holy Spirit in her life. Remember principle number 1?

7. *Prayer provides the power for change.* As a discipleship coaching partner, you must become a prayer warrior, interceding for your partner with passion and purpose. If you are not yet comfortable praying aloud with others, this may become an area of growth for you.

8. *Accountability is a key component of a coaching relationship.* The coaching partners help each other set goals and action steps. Then they ask follow-up questions, which increase the likelihood of their reaching those goals.

9. *Encouragement is essential.* The kind of encouragement the New Testament Greek describes is not necessarily the "pat on the back" type of encouragement but rather encouraging her to persevere despite her feeling of discouragement.

10. *Celebration is the ultimate delight of a coaching relationship.* It is an intentional time of rejoicing with your partner as she overcomes bondage from the past, experiences spiritual breakthroughs, redeems damaged relationships, and reaches new heights of love and obedience to her Lord.

Coaching Conversations

THREE TYPES OF COACHING QUESTIONS

1. Open Questions

OPEN QUESTIONS ARE the primary format of a coaching conversation. They are inquiry questions that cannot be answered with a simple "yes" or "no" and usually give the partner an opportunity to determine the direction of the discussion, instead of the coach directing it.

Examples:

> ➢ What has been going on in your life since the last time we talked?
> ➢ What issue would you like to discuss today?
> ➢ How did you handle that?
> ➢ How would you do things differently if you had a "do over"?

2. Direct Questions

A direct question is more focused and comes later in the conversation, after the partner has narrowed the focus of the discussion.

Examples:

- ➢ What do you intend to do about the situation?
- ➢ When do you plan to address it?
- ➢ Is there someone who needs to be involved in that decision?
- ➢ What is the ideal outcome?

3. Reflective Questions

Reflective questions give the partner a chance to go deeper in her thought process, tapping into her soul and spirit.

Examples:

- ➢ Has the Lord given you any new insights in your study this week?
- ➢ What do you think He is saying to you through that scripture?
- ➢ What do you believe is at the core of that attitude?
- ➢ What would be God's best outcome for you in that situation?
- ➢ In what way does that response reflect the character of Christ?

CAUTIONS

Make sure you are sensitive to any judgmental attitude or critical spirit as you think through your questions. Your coaching partner will sense it quickly and may become defensive and begin to build up a barrier to authentic communication.

Do not use solution-oriented questions. They are just your advice disguised as questions. For example, "Have you thought about setting up an appointment to talk with your pastor?" The advice is: "Set up an appointment with your pastor." Even if you think this is the best way for her to move forward, a better way to phrase that question might be, "Is there someone you trust who might have a different perspective on this situation and can help you think it through?" Though it is a direct question, and somewhat solution-oriented, it is less controlling.

Coaching Covenant

BELIEVING THAT GOD is at work in your life, I choose to partner with you and the Holy Spirit on this path toward the "crucified life."

I will:

- Always be real with you.
- Always hold everything in confidence.
- Never give you advice.
- Never promote my own agenda for you.
- Challenge you but never judge or criticize you.
- Pray for you regularly.
- Help hold you accountable to the goals and action steps you have chosen.
- Encourage your progress.
- Celebrate your success.

Today, _____ (date), I enter into this covenant with

_____, trusting God to do immeasurably more than we

could ask or imagine as we seek a deeper intimacy with Him, a greater obedience to His Word,

and a more faithful ministry in His world.

Coaching partner _____

Coaching partner_____

Search the Scriptures

(For Part Two)

WORLDVIEW

Proverbs 9:10
Proverbs 21:31
1 Corinthians 1:20
1 Corinthians 3:19
Colossians 2:8
John 15:19

Romans 12:2
John 17:14, 16
1 John 5:4–5
Titus 2:11–13
Colossians 2:2–3
Ephesians 2:1–3

WOUNDS

Luke 6:43–45
John 3:19
1 Corinthians 1:3–4
Acts 26:17–18
Ephesians 5:8–9
Mark 11:25

Matthew 6:14–15
Luke 6:37
Ephesians 4:31–32
Colossians 3:12–14
1 John 5:7
1 John 2:9–11

WANTS

Ecclesiastes 6:9

Psalms 119:36–37

Psalms 73:25b

Galatians 5:16

Matthew 6:19

Matthew 6:21

1 Timothy 6:6–10

Romans 13:8

Acts 4:32–35

Acts 20:33–35

Matthew 19:21

Philippians 3:8

WILL

Psalms 86:11

Psalms 143:10

John 6:38–40

John 4:34

Romans 12:2

John 9:31

Matthew 7:21

Mark 3:35

1 John 2:17

Hebrews 13:20–21

Hebrews 10:35

Philippians 2:12–13

Romans 8:26–27

Colossians 1:9

1 John 5:14

1 Thessalonians 4:3

1 Thessalonians 5:16

Ephesians 5:17

CRUCIFIED LIFE

Romans 6:1–11

2 Corinthians 4:10

2 Corinthians 6:16–7:1

Galatians 5:24

Galatians 6:14

Ephesians 4:22–24

Colossians 2:20

Colossians 3:5

Colossians 3:9–10

Certificate of Death

I, _____ , have been crucified with Christ, and I no longer live, but Christ lives in me. The life I now live in the body I live by faith in the Son of God, Who loved me and gave Himself for me. I know that my old self was crucified with Him.

I am no longer a slave to sin, and I will live in it no longer. Just as Christ was raised from the dead through the glory of the Father, I too may live a new life. As one who belongs to Christ Jesus, I have crucified the sinful nature with its passions and desires. I have taken off my old self and have put on the new self, which is being renewed in the image of my Creator.

Today, I claim the truth that His divine power has given me everything I need for life and godliness, through my knowledge of Him, Who has called me by His own glory and goodness. Therefore, I am able to participate in the divine nature and escape the corruption of the world. Through the Holy Spirit, I have been given fullness in Christ, Who is the head over every power and authority.

I accept the truth that my body is a temple of the living God; therefore, I purify myself from everything that contaminates body and spirit, perfecting holiness out of reverence for God.

May I never boast except in the cross of our Lord Jesus Christ, through which the world has been crucified to me and I to the world.

Date_____

Scripture references: Galatians 2:20; 5:24; 6:14; Romans 6:1–11; Colossians 3:9–10; 2 Peter 1:3–4; 2 Corinthians 6:16; 7:1

Endnotes

Introduction

1. From the epilogue, by editor Gene Edwards, in Jeanne Guyon, *Experiencing the Depths of Jesus Christ* (Jacksonville, FL: SeedSowers Publishing, 1975), 150.
2. A. W. Tozer, *The Root of the Righteous* (Camp Hill, PA: Christian Publications, 1986), 49.
3. Wesley L. Duewel, *Measure Your Life* (Grand Rapids, MI: Zondervan Publishing, 1992), 186.

Chapter 5

1. A. W. Tozer, *The Root of the Righteous* (Camp Hill, PA: Christian Publications, 1986), 63.
2. A. W. Tozer, *Gems from Tozer: Selections from the Writings of A. W. Tozer* (Camp Hill, PA: Christian Publications, 1979), 35–36.

Chapter 9

1. Richard Foster, *Freedom of Simplicity* (San Francisco, CA: Harper & Row, 1989), 3.

Chapter 12

1. Dan Allender, *To Be Told: God Invites You to Coauthor Your Future* (Colorado Springs, CO: WaterBrook Press, 2005), 1.
2. Ibid., 3.
3. L. E. Maxwell, *Born Crucified* (Chicago, IL: Moody Publishers, 1945, 2002, 2010), 34.

Part 2

1. Kenneth Boa, *Conformed to His Image: Biblical approaches to Spiritual Formation* (Grand Rapids, MI: Zondervan, 2001), 424.

Chapter 13

1. Tim LaHaye, David Noebel, *Mind Siege* (Nashville, TN: Word Publishing, 2000), 35.
2. Ibid., 124–129.
3. David Jeremiah, *Invasion of Other Gods: The Seduction of New Age Spirituality* (Dallas, TX: Thomas Nelson, 1995), 21–22.
4. Ibid.
5. Ibid.
6. Ibid., 23.
7. Ibid., 24.
8. Ibid., 24–25.
9. www.acim.org
10. John Ankerberg, John Weldon, *Encyclopedia of New Age Beliefs* (Eugene, OR: Harvest House Publishers, 1996), 1.
11. Ibid., 2.
12. Rhonda Byrne, *The Secret* (Hillsboro, OR: Beyond Words Publishing, 2006), 7.
13. Ibid., 9.
14. Ibid., 10.
15. Ibid., 11.
16. Ibid., 98–99.
17. Ibid., 130.
18. Chip Ingram, *The Invisible War: What Every Believer Needs to Know About Satan, Demons, and Spiritual Warfare* (Grand Rapids, MI: Baker Books, 2006), 37.
19. Neil Anderson, Rich Miller, Paul Travis, *Breaking the Bondage of Legalism* (Eugene, OR: Harvest House Publishers, 2003), 8.
20. Ibid., 68.
21. Ibid., 37–38.
22. George Barna, *Growing True Disciples* (Colorado Springs, CO: WaterBrook Press, 2001), 11.

Chapter 14

1. Dan Allendar, *The Wounded Heart: Hope for Adult Victims of Childhood Sexual Abuse* (Colorado Springs, CO: NavPress, 2008), 14.
2. Ibid., 183.

3. Brennan Manning, *Abba's Child: The Cry of the Heart for Intimate Belonging* (Colorado Springs, CO: NavPress, 1994), 151.
4. Dan Allendar, *The Wounded Heart: Hope for Adult Victims of Childhood Sexual Abuse* (Colorado Springs, CO: NavPress, 2008), 175.
5. A. W. Tozer, *The Root of the Righteous* (Camp Hill, PA: Christian Publications, 1986), 13.
6. Stephen F. Olford, *Not I but Christ* (Wheaton, IL: Crossway Books, 1995), 136.
7. Neil Anderson, *The Bondage Breaker* (Eugene, OR: Harvest House Publishers, 2000), 27.
8. A. W. Tozer, *The Root of the Righteous* (Camp Hill, PA: Christian Publications, 1986), 112.

Chapter 15

1. Kenneth Boa, *Conformed to His Image: Biblical approaches to Spiritual Formation* (Grand Rapids, MI: Zondervan, 2001), 285.
2. Richard Foster, *Freedom of Simplicity* (San Francisco, CA: Harper & Row, 1989), 104–105.
3. A. W. Tozer, *The Root of the Righteous* (Camp Hill, PA: Christian Publications, 1986), 116–118.

Chapter 16

1. Keith Drury, *Holiness for Ordinary People* (Indianapolis, IN: Wesleyan Publishing House, 1994), 92–93.
2. Charles Finney, *The Spirit-Filled Life* (New Kensington, PA: Whitaker House, 1999), 78.
3. Kenneth Boa, *Conformed to His Image: Biblical approaches to Spiritual Formation* (Grand Rapids, MI: Zondervan, 2001), 104.
4. V. Raymond Edman, *They Found the Secret* (Grand Rapids, MI: Zondervan, 1984), 186–188.
5. Andrew Murray, *Abide in Christ: The Joy of Being in God's Presence* (New Kensington, PA: Whitaker House, 1979), 23–24.
6. A. W. Tozer, *The Root of the Righteous* (Camp Hill, PA: Christian Publications, 1986), 156.

Part Three

1. Jeanne Guyon, *Experiencing the Depths of Jesus Christ* (Jacksonville, FL: SeedSowers Publishing, 1975), 45.

Chapter 18

1. Keith Drury, *Holiness for Ordinary People* (Indianapolis, IN: Wesleyan Publishing House, 1994), 13–14.
2. Howard Hendricks, William Hendricks, *Living By the Book* (Chicago, IL: Moody Press, 1991), 9.

3. John MacArthur, *How to Study the Bible* (Chicago, IL: Moody Publishers, 2009), 15–16.
4. George Barna, *Growing True Disciples* (Colorado Springs, CO: WaterBrook Press, 2001), 71.
5. Ibid.
6. Norman L. Geisler, Paul K. Hoffman, Editors, *Why I am a Christian: Leading Thinkers Explain Why They Believe* (Grand Rapids, MI: Baker Books, 2006), 159.
7. Warren Wiersbe, *The Bible Exposition Commentary: The Prophets Isaiah–Malachi* (Colorado Springs, CO: David C. Cook, 2002), 285.
8. Adele Ahlberg Calhoun, *Spiritual Disciplines Handbook: Practices that Transforms Us* (Downers Grove, IL: InterVarsity Press, 2005), 57.

Chapter 19

1. E. M. Bounds, *Thy Will Be Done* (New Kensington, PA: Whitaker House, 2000), 9.
2. E. M. Bounds, *On Prayer* (New Kensington, PA: Whitaker House, 1997), 31.
3. Ibid., 27.
4. Bob Sorge, *Secrets of the Secret Place* (Lee's Summit, MO: Oasis House, 2001), 32.
5. Ibid., 28.
6. E. M. Bounds, *On Prayer* (New Kensington, PA: Whitaker House, 1997), 22.
7. E. M. Bounds, *Thy Will Be Done* (New Kensington, PA: Whitaker House, 2000), 24.
8. Ibid., 79.

Chapter 20

1. Warren Wiersbe, *The Bible Exposition Commentary: The Prophets Isaiah–Malachi* (Colorado Springs, CO: David C. Cook, 2002), 481.
2. Dallas Willard, *The Spirit of the Disciplines: Understanding How God Changes Lives* (New York, NY: HarperCollins Publishers, 1988), 161.
3. Richard Foster, *Celebration of Discipline* (New York, NY: Harper Collins Publishers, 1998), 159.

Chapter 21

1. Kenneth Boa, *Conformed to His Image: Biblical approaches to Spiritual Formation* (Grand Rapids, MI: Zondervan, 2001), 368.
2. A. W. Tozer, *Success and the Christian: The Cost of Spiritual Maturity* (Camp Hill, PA: Christian Publications, 1994), 88.
3. Ibid., 89.
4. Charles Colson, Ellen Vaughn, *Being the Body* (Nashville, TN: W Publishing Group, 2003), 87.

5. Kenneth Boa, *Conformed to His Image: Biblical approaches to Spiritual Formation* (Grand Rapids, MI: Zondervan, 2001), 365.

6. Ibid., 368.

7. Paul J. Achtemeier, *General Editor Harper's Bible Dictionary* (San Francisco, CA: Harper & Row Publishers, 1985), 1078.

8. George Barna, "New Study Shows Trends in Tithing and Donating," www.barna.org, (Accessed April 14, 2008).

9. Craig Groeschel, *Chazown* (Sisters, OR: Multnomah Publishers, 2006), 158.

10. Ibid., 154.

11. Michael Kendrick, Ben Ortlip, *Blueprint for Life: Discovering the Life You Were Born to Live* (Blueprint for Life, Inc., 2004), 87.

12. Os Guiness, *The Call* (Nashville, TN: Word Publishing, 1998), 31.

13. Ibid.

14. Ibid., 49–50.

15. Ibid., 46.

16. Craig Groeschel, *Chazown* (Sisters, OR: Multnomah Publishers, 2006), 49.

17. Bill & Amy Stearns, *2020 Vision* (Minneapolis, MN: Bethany House, 2005), 66.

18. Warren Wiersbe, *On Being a Servant of God* (Grand Rapids, MI: Baker Books, 2007), 12.

19. Jo Anne Lyon, *The Ultimate Blessing: Rediscovering the Power of God's Presence* (Indianapolis, IN: Wesleyan Publishing House, 2003), 171.

20. Ibid., 174.

Part Four

1. E. M. Bounds, *On Prayer* (New Kensington, PA: Whitaker House, 1997), 342.

Chapter 23

1. Jack Lannom, *Untapped Potential: Turning Ordinary People into Extraordinary Performers* (Nashville, TN: Thomas Nelson Publishers, 1998), 157.

2. Jane A. G. Kise, David Stark, Sandra Krebs Hirsh, *Discover Who you Are* (Minneapolis, MN: Bethany House, 2005), 182.

Chapter 24

1. John Avant, *The Passion Promise: Living a Life Only God Can Imagine* (Sisters, OR: Multnomah Publishers, 2004), 170.

Chapter 26

1. Kenneth Boa, *Conformed to His Image: Biblical approaches to Spiritual Formation* (Grand Rapids, MI: Zondervan, 2001), 306.
2. Adapted from www.mintools.com.
3. Don & Katie Fortune, *Discover Your God-Given Gifts* (Grand Rapids, MI: Chosen Books, 1987), 15.
4. Ibid., 16.
5. Ibid., 17.

Chapter 27

1. Wayne Cordeiro, *The Dream Releasers* (Ventura, CA: Regal Books, 2002), 50.

Chapter 28

1. Charles R. Swindoll, *Living Above the Level of Mediocrity: A Commitment to Excellence* (Waco, TX: Word Books, 1987), 276.

Chapter 29

1. Anne Graham Lotz, *I Saw The Lord* (Grand Rapids, MI: Zondervan, 2006), 91.
2. Ibid., 92.

Appendix 1
Coaching Principles and Practices

1. George Barna, *Growing True Disciples* (Colorado Springs, CO: WaterBrook Press, 2001), 11.
2. Ibid., 36.
3. Richard Foster, *Celebration of Discipline* (New York, NY: Harper Collins Publishers, 1998), 10.

CPSIA information can be obtained at www.ICGtesting.com
Printed in the USA
BVOW041334150312

285122BV00003B/3/P